ABOUT THE AUTH

As founder and director of Family Caring Trust Michael Quinn made a pioneering contribution to parent support in Britain and Ireland. In **an article in the *Guardian* on Parenting Sharon Maxwell Magnus tells how she asked the chief professional officer for the Health Visitors' Association, "What book would you recommend for parents – by Penelope Leach, Sheila Kitzinger, Dr Spock, Chris Green...?"**

"None," the officer replied, "they all make parents feel guilty. But if you were to ask me who was doing the most effective work in helping parents, it would have to be Michael Quinn, director of Family Caring."

Under a photo of Michael and his wife Terri, the headline of an *Irish Times* article read, 'A Place in Parenting History' (May 1996).

The courses Michael designed with his wife Terri reached over half a million parents in the UK alone; his books have sold over two million copies and been translated into eighteen languages.

In his retirement Michael wrote this book about his childhood in Armagh. If you ever wondered what childhood events might lead someone to become a social reformer, you may be none the wiser after reading 'An Armagh Childhood.' Here is a picture of a wilful, lonely child – who could have done with a parenting programme!

It is not Michael's first sally into creative writing. In the nineteen sixties and seventies he published 'Dance to Democracy,' a collection of satirical 'broadsides,' he was Northern Ireland columnist for Ireland's humorous magazine, Dublin Opinion, and he had occasional appearances on BBC and Radio Éireann reading some of his own writing and singing his own satirical songs. Creative writing stopped with the demands of parenting and work.

AN ARMAGH CHILDHOOD

the story of the little boy

in the small Irish town

Michael Quinn

First published July 2013
by Family Caring Trust
© Michael Quinn June 2013

New revised edition September 2013
Published by Createspace.com
© Michael Quinn August 2013

ISBN: 978-1-872253-23-7

All profits from this book go to the charity *Family Caring Trust*, 44 Rathfriland Road, Newry, Co. Down, Northern Ireland BT34 1LD.

Many charities focus on children, but a focus on supporting parents can often be more effective. Family Caring is the parent-support charity which Michael founded and directed for twenty-five years. It continues to offer effective support to parents across the world.

The book is only available from Amazon or Family Caring Trust. Consider recommending rather than loaning it to friends as Family Caring benefits from all sales.

The picture on the cover is of the hill of Armagh, crowned by the Church of Ireland cathedral and with some suggestion of a mediaeval fortress. It was painted by Michael Quinn's niece Máire Quinn, a talented artist whose awards include the Elizabeth Scott-Moore Royal Society Watercolour Award 2001.

It was on this symbolic hill, where St Patrick founded the Irish Church, that Michael Quinn was reared.

DEDICATION

To my parents, Mick and Ciss,

whom I now deeply appreciate.

Author's note to revised edition.

I have been gratified by the success of the first edition of this book. It was a rushed publication, however, because I was in poor health and my doctors thought I did not have long to live. I think there was some very good writing in the book, but there were also some rushed, poorly-written parts. Thanks to the intervention of a very skilled surgeon, I have been given time to improve those passages somewhat in this edition.

Some people have commented that I make myself very vulnerable in the book, but a good memoir is not to boast and brag about what a great fella I am. I suspect that any decent memoir may demand quite radical honesty. I trust that this new edition will give greater pleasure to my readers.

CONTENTS

IMPORTANT: BEFORE YOU BEGIN...

THIS IS MY MEMORY of a childhood growing up in Armagh, occasionally filling in gaps with my siblings' memories. My goal in writing is to let you taste a morsel of Armagh in its cultural setting but chiefly to tell the story of a sensitive, wilful, lonely, imaginative, generous – and often selfish – child who has been inculturated into this unique time and place. Even a chapter like 'My Parents' is not so much about my parents as about the child – all part of my development of the child's story.

I write in the present tense to make it more immediate: each piece is written as if I had no awareness of the future. In that way I try to convey my impressions, my prejudices, my inculturation, at each stage of the journey. My working life, for example, has brought me into close contact and friendship with Protestants in all the mainstream Protestant churches in Britain and Ireland. It may be important to bear this in mind as you meet the deep prejudices against Protestants described here as part of my childhood mind. The cruelty to insects and animals that I describe was also part of my childhood culture and is something I now deplore. My early dismissal of my parents has long given way to a deep appreciation. And my reaction to St Patrick's College says much more about me than about the college –the staff without exception were fair and I was never aware of any hint of abuse. Finally, the faults I found with my friends and my inability to form friendships had obviously nothing to do with the friends themselves and everything to do with my own inadequacy in developing relationships.

I have changed the names of only a few people – just in those few instances where I felt it was better to protect their identity.

I am particularly grateful to my siblings for their support in putting the book together, especially to my sister Brenda, herself a poet, whose tips on style were invaluable. I owe most to Mel McMahon for his support and encouragement – Mel has considerable writing ability in his own right and has also published a number of poets through Abbey Press.

EARLY DAYS

I am born on the eighteenth of April 1941, the sixth child in the family. Dr Sheils weighs me with his eye, "You'd think Mick had sput this chil' out of his mouth." So they call me Michael after my daddy.

It is the night of the great German blitz on Belfast. That is nothing to me. I have replaced my sister Brenda at mammy's breast, a cuckoo taking over her nest. I don't remember, but my body tells me that I wallowed in mammy's milky pillows and boozed on breast, soothed by the gurgles and heart-beats from beneath her warm skin.

We live over our baby shop at number ten, Ogle Street. A maid, Sara, cares for me because mammy and daddy are busy in their other draper's shop across the street, number thirteen.

"I love every bit of him," Sara declares, "every wee bit of him."

DOOM COMES in late September of 1942: mammy appears with my new baby brother Victor. He sucks where I'm supposed to suck: I hate him.

The months move on. I see the coal bucket and slither across, bellying myself over the floor to pat the cold metal and mouth a greeting. I taste coal bits and spit them out. I chew wood chips until Sara screams, "The rascal!" and, giggling, hoists me away...

Daddy is irked and fussy around the others, then turns to me.

"Who's a great boy?" he smiles, "Who's the best man in the house – well..? There's only the two Michaels – eh?"

When Sara changes my nappy, he plays wolf, barking 'aaaaghrrrr' into my bare chest, eating me up with his wide-open, spitty mouth, his jaggy cheeks, his gruff, bristled chin. He sucks and tickles me, forcing chuckles out of me. I don't like it. I wish he would stop.

"LOOK AT THAT lovely curl!" Sara smiles. "Handsome boy! Where did you get such a gorgeous curl? Will you give it to me?"

"No. My cuwl."

Brenda has straight hair.

"Here. Into this room – I need to tidy your curl."

She coaxes me into the bathroom, stands me in front of the mirror.

We're not allowed to touch daddy's black-handled cut-throat razor. I watch as Brenda climbs onto the lavatory bowl to reach it down from the shelf.

"Hold steady. Don't move."

Trim as a nurse, she slices my curl clean off.

"Lovely boy, Michael. See yourself in the mirror."

My curl is gone. I like having straight hair like her.

I watch her clip my curl onto her hair, centre forehead.

Smiling, she leads me downstairs – to family outrage, shouting and raw beating.

This photo of my mother (pregnant with Eugene), my father and the staff was taken (early 1944) in front of our shop at 13 Ogle Street.

ONE WEEK AFTER MY THIRD BIRTHDAY, a new baby, Eugene, arrives. No warning.

"He's beautiful, Missus Quinn. Aw, the wee face."

It's lies. Can't they see his face is squashed, patchy-red – a bit like the pink babies we saw in the rat's nest near the shuck. Now I have two brothers I hate.

Sara bumps Eugene up Ogle Street in our hand-me-down pram. She pushes off, me walking beside her gripping the metal handle.

I sniff a faint mouldy smell from John Cassidy standing at his door. We pass little stone houses with their doors open. Maisie Grimes is kneeling in one doorway washing the doorstep:

15

"Well, Sara," she smiles. "Is this boy behaving hisself?"

"Deed he is. Deed he is."

My eyes sparkle at the sight of Sandy MacPherson's donkey and cart parked in front of his greengrocer's shop. Onto the cart Sandy has loaded brown sacks of potatoes, wooden boxes of apples, loose turnips and cabbages. He bundles an armful of stringed carrots onto the back, smiles "Hello, Miss," and hops up two steps into his shop. Flies buzz around his donkey's eyes and bum. Its tail sways and swishes at them. Its head is bent low wishing for grass. It turns its big nostrils towards me, its eyes blank, wondering about me.

"Is the donkey sad, Sara?"

"Oh, such a question, chil'! Sure how do I know what donkeys feel? Though I betcha he's not that happy – I wudden like flies pesterin' at me all day."

"Where does it sleep at night?"

"I dunno. Sure I suppose a field."

I'd hate to be a donkey. Sleeping out in the cold. Flies buzzin' at me. I'm glad I'm just me.

Sara jostles on over the cobbles at the arch into Kirker's lemonade works. Bottles sing in the crates, clinking, jangling, announcing lemonade above the growl of a lorry.

We bounce on up to the inky paper smell of Bennett's Stationers and Printers, we nudge around the stone steps at McKee's grocery, push on by Hughie Trainor's sweetie shop and past a huge clomping horse pulling a cart of coal bags, the wheels chattering to one another and to the street. I stare at the driver's bogeyman face – only the wrinkles at his eyes are still skin. I'm afraid of coalmen.

Three men are grouped at the corner smoking. They don't look at each other, just glance up and back along the street while they talk.

"Why are men always standin' there, Sara?"

"Och, they're corner-boys, chil'. They've no jobs."

We round the corner into Lower Irish Street. Frank Toner is polishing the chrome rim of his taxi with a torn cloth.

"Hello... there, Miss... It's like more rain."

"Ye wudden know what it'd do, Mister Toner. I better turn roun' soon 'fore it gets heavy."

She sallies on.

"What's the smelly stink, Sara?"

"Tha's just cabbage water, chil'. Somebody's boilin' cabbage for their dinner."

Missus Starrs, the church sacristan, is footering her key into the door but leaves it to goo at Eugene, then notice me.

"Michael's some size! He's grew up all of a sudden. Don't be spoilin' him now – I doubt she's spoilin' you, is she, Michael?"

"Naw, no spoilin' at all, Missus Starrs. He's a good chil', so he is."

Sara blesses herself outside St Malachy's church.

"We were goin' to go in for a wee visit to God, but this rain's comin' on heavier."

She twists the pram round to face back. Frank Toner is still rubbing at his taxi in light rain.

"I doubt the rain has us bate," he grunts.

Back into Ogle Street, Sara stops a moment to chat to Missus McGreevey. I gaze up at the deepening drizzle as it creeps down a window in dusty trickles, then darts down to the cracked putty at the bottom of the pane before dribbling into the window-sill and weeping muddy slobbers onto the footpath. I blink at shadows slipping past me of cloth-capped men and head-scarfed women. I gawk up at rusty downpipes holding up roofs, at clouds gathering and drifting across the Armagh sky. Wide-eyed girls bend into the pram to smile at Eugene. Scary, staring old women goo at him too. I wish they would go away. I'm standing too long.

"Can we not go home now, Sara," I gern.

I PLAY SHOP on the dirt path beside mammy's cabbages, brussels sprouts and everlasting onions. Our money is broken scraps of delph dug out of the dirt. A pile of plain white pieces is worth little. With bits of delph we buy from each other pretty pieces with traces of flower or willow on them. We pay dear for a stump of teapot or a scrap of old cup with a friendly trace of colour. Best are the chips of china, especially a splinter with gold edging. I store my treasures in an old saucepan and wash them with my thumbs in dirty rain water.

We find a dead, curled-up slater. Pat says it's a wood-louse, but its wrinkled back is the colour of a slate and you find them under old slates. It lies on its back, shrivelled legs fallen aside. Anne says to give it a funeral.

For a coffin we use the black crinkley top of a Dettol bottle and drop the corpse slowly into that. We turn to collecting mourners for the procession to the graveyard, searching under stones and gathering a cluster of live slaters into a jam-jar. Brenda finds an earywig and a Hairy Mary and adds them in. They

18

look frightened: it fascinates me to see them wriggle and suffer in this strange jumble. The slaters attempt to crawl and clamber over one another's long shoulders, their legs and whiskers churning, making a wobbly, seething mass at the bottom of the jar.

We line the route to the slater's grave with twigs, and Brenda slowly moves the Dettol coffin along this path. Everyone holds a stick as we spill out our squirming congregation of two, three, four… more and more slaters into the narrow funeral passageway. The slaters want to scurry away but our sticks keep moving them along in the procession. Some rebel and escape to a crushing shoe. Our row of security tightens with screamed alerts and excited yelps.

Pat takes over, gently placing the Dettol top into a small, deep grave and closing it over with sticky, blackberry-like soil that also buries some mourners. The rest of the mourners seek out the nearest shadows. Pat says that earywigs are called earywigs because they like to curl up inside your ear. I make sure this one won't: I crush it with a stone.

I MISS SARA. Nobody said she was going away. Missus Early comes to help in the kitchen. She lipsticks her lips with blotchy smudges of red ink that go up near her nose. She gives me porridge in a tin mug. When I'm finished, she pours tea into the same mug without cleaning it. I'll vomit if I drink the tea. I leave it.

At dinner-time we eat shepherd's pie from a big enamel dish in the middle of the table. I hate the others burrowing into my square of champ: I don't want their spit on my food. The worst part of any dinner is stalks of cabbage. I slip them out of my mouth and scatter them under the table. When they're found, everyone is scolded for 'wasting good food.'

Missus Early doesn't stay, but the new maid, Ivy, is bossy. She never cuddles.

"Come on, hurry up, get them shoes off! Don't take all day. Do you think I've nothin' better to do! God's keeping an eye on you, mister, and writing your sins intill a notebook, givin' you black marks for laziness. He sees everythin' – you can't fool him!"

THERE IS A MATRESS in the long hallway. Gerard and Pat are lunging pillows past it, then chairs, holy pictures, towels, armfuls of clothes as big as themselves.

Daddy's voice is raised. "Careful! Watch the wall! Ahhh… Look, you're scraping the paint. I cautioned you, but you don't listen!"

"Sure I can't see!" Pat grumbles. "This is far too big a load"

"Did I tell you to take that much! No, but you had to do it your way – you had to scrape the wall!"

All morning the moving forges on. Along the corridor, down the stairs, through the baby-clothes shop, out into the street. From the upstairs room I peer, baffled. I feel my world changing, but no one explains. I see them crisscross Ogle Street, their bundles swallowed into our other shop at number thirteen, daddy still fussing and heckling like a goose.

"Watch out crossing the street. You can't be too careful. Gerard, what are you doing? Where's Pat gone? Why's Pat not helpin'?"

20

Finally it's our turn. The new maid, Ivy, pulls me and Victor, our hands grabbed tight, across the street, through the long shop, up the wooden steps at the back. We have tea-time in a pokey, dark kitchen. I am seated at the little table, hunkered in beside the stopped clock on the window-sill. I bite gorilla bites out of my bread and jam and pause to examine the teeth marks. Ivy tells me 'hurry up.' I slurp down a mug of tea. Our only toilet is in the yard outside. Ivy unbuttons me, I close the door and perch up on the bowl, clutching like a hen, fearful of falling in. I wipe myself with cut-up sheets of newspaper. Ivy comes in and pulls the chain. I scowl, stiff and frightened, at the explosion of water surging around the bowl from a rusty tank bolstered up near the ceiling.

"What'll happen if the water floods out?" I ask.

"Never you mind. Curiosity killed the cat. Come on. Time for bed!"

I climb the stairs from the dark kitchen. My older brothers and sisters will still sleep across the street in our old home, but there are two bedrooms here, an inside one for mammy and daddy, and for Eugene in his cot; in the other room the bed at the wall is for Victor and me. I'm relieved I'm not sleeping next the wall – Pat says night mares come out of there, scary ghost-horses.

Two holy pictures hang on nails. One saint with a sweet, red-lipped face has a bright cloud at the back of her head, and her eyes look glumly up sideways to heaven. She's hoping she doesn't have to stay a minute longer on this grim earth. I think the other saint is God. He's cross and frowns down. Ivy says I'm a 'bad rascal' and God's angry eyes agree with her. He was never meant to look at the likes of me;

he knows what's inside me and follows me with those accusing, disappointed eyes into every corner of the room. He can't see me when I stoop behind the bed board, but he's waiting to glower at me once I stick my head back up. I'm ashamed. I feel guilty about being bad, letting him down.

Ivy comes up the stairs, turns off the gas mantle and goes away, leaving the dark behind. I can't sleep. The moon is shining through the two small skylight windows, forcing shadows to creep close to my quilt. I feel a ghost looking at me. I need to use the potty, but I'm afraid to get out of bed. I have to go. I crawl out, pull the delph potty out from under the bed and listen to myself peeing, a thin streaming sound becoming splashier. That'll scare a ghost away, I hope. In the morning, the room is bright, the skylights just dull and rusty. This is where we live now.

EVERYONE'S COAT HANGS on hooks in the hallway, crushed damp against the wall when you open our back door. You've to squeeze past the pram to get to the door. Ivy puts Victor and Eugene into the pram and pushes it out the door.

"Hold the door open till I get the pram out," she snaps. "Wide! Wide! Mind!"

From the back-yard, she heads through our long entry, a broken stone wall on our left, the steep, high-reaching wall of Saint Malachy's School on the right.

"Hold on to the pram and don't let it go."

We pass Mary Coo-Coo's half-door. Nobody knows her real name but we sense she's a half-witch. We've figured that out this long time, for she mutters away to herself over the half-door and has a hump on

her back and a mug of water ready to throw at the
boys who bang her door at night. She scares me. I'm
glad she's not at her door now.

We proceed down Chapel Lane to Red Ned's pub
at the corner into Ogle Street.

"I can't hold the pram – the footpath's too
short."

"You're a nuisance! Walk behind and hold the
tail of my coat."

Paddy McKee is standing in his doorway,
wrapped in a barber's apron.

"That chil' is his daddy's son. He's a great wee
man."

"Aw now," Ivy replies as she rolls on by.

Past Hanratty's with the boxes of cornflakes in
the window. Past our drapery with plastic women
modelling clothes in the shop window and staring
away out like they don't care.

Now Tom Hill the cooper's shop. His wooden
barrels are out on show on the footpath. I can't hold
on to Ivy's coat as she struggles the pram around the
barrels.

"They shouldn't allow that," she grumbles,
"blocking the whole footpath."

Danny McShane has also cluttered the footpath.
Two half-fixed bicycles are tilted against his window-
silll, an upside-down one stuck in next to them with
the wheel spinning. Danny's hands are greasy with
dirt. He must have no mammy.

"Morning, Danny," Ivy beams, "hard at work!"

Danny tosses his black curls back and looks
sideways.

"Ah... sure..." he grunts, "you have to be doin'
somethin'. At least the rain's holdin' off." I wonder
why his face is suddenly all red.

Past the post office, we turn into Thomas Street.
I goggle at Missus Hamill's shop window: huge glass
jars of sweets grin out at me. The faint whiff of
brandy balls stirs an empty longing in me.

The pram twists into Jack McKenna's chemist
shop. Jack's brother wheezes a wintry smile at Ivy.

"It's cold."

"It is, Mister McKenna, very coul'. Will it ever
warm up I dunno. Have you a cough mixture for this
chil'? He's been barkin' a cough all night and Missus
Quinn wondered would you give 'im somethin'."

"Oh, we'll have to look after him... Give him a
spoonful of this three times a day after meals and he'll
be right as rain."

"Thanks, Mister McKenna. Michael, will you hol'
the door open for me like a good chil'."

She only says my name and talks polite when
someone big is around.

I'M NOT WELL.

"There's divil all wrong wi' you," Ivy snaps.
"Always lookin' for notice!"

The next morning I have a temperature and
German Measles. They cover the skylights to darken
the room.

"You have to stay in the dark or you'll go blind,"
I'm told.

I'm glad to be special. German Measles sounds
important. Mammy gives me a soft kiss before she
does down to the shop for the day.

Ivy brings me a hot drink of lemons and sugar:

"If you spill a drop o' this I'll skin you! I'm sick, sore and tired between bringin' you up stuff an' luggin' your potty down the stairs! I've got me own work to do!"

I look up at the dim, darkened ceiling of off-white, tongued-and-grooved boards. With my eyes I join up the rusty nails and the lines of the wood. Ships and mountains and horses take shape above me, then monsters with scary beaks and bulging eyes. Some glare down cross at me. I lookaway but they still keep staring at me out of the ceiling. I don't want to have measles anymore...

IVY STEERS ME across the town. Past Mallocca's that churns out sliders and pokes of home-made Italian ice-cream. We pass Forte's chip shop: they sell chips in newspaper that is curled into a poke. They must buy an awful lot of newspapers. She leads me past the friendly, winking-at-me lights of Woolworths and down to Missus McCormick's nursery school in Railway Street. Missus McCormick's face is full of her cheeks and a mass of wrinkles from old age and smiling. Her eyes bulge behind thick glasses. They sparkle at me.

"You're a great boy, Michael," she greets me, "and you walked the whole way down here."

"He's aw'right, Missus McCormick," Ivy interrupts, "I hope yiz can put a bit o' manners on him while he's here."

She goes off and Missus McCormick hangs up my coat beside a picture of an elephant.

"That'll be your sign, the elephant, Michael, and this is your blanket with an elephant sewn onto it for when you take your nap."

I stand cowed in a big room, watching strange boys and girls playing and running. I listen to their talk making peculiar echoes into the roof. I drink orange and eat cut-funny sandwiches. In the afternoon I lie covered in my elephant blanket, but it's too strange and too marvellous to sleep.

Soon I chant nursery rhymes and build up blocks with other boys and girls and I twirl plasticine into pink snakes and green worms. I love here.

THERE'S A WAR SOMEWHERE. People don't talk about it for fear of scaring us. Their voices drop, thinking I can't hear the whispers. They only speak a few words like 'cancer,' 'TB,' and 'Hitler' with that hush. Some of my sisters are sent off to aunts in the country to keep them safe from bombs. I'd rather be here at home in our cosy dining-room.

There's a framed picture of Pope Pius on the dining-room wall. He's praying out his blessing onto mammy and daddy's wedding anniversary. I feel important and proud that the pope took the trouble to send us this. On the opposite wall is a picture of Jesus that scares me. He's God and he has a moustache and a beard and long hair. His heart has come out in front of him to let us see the thorns sticking into it. There's a burning flame at the top. You're not allowed to take his name in vain – that means you're not supposed to say his name without bowing your chin into your neck. Like the picture upstairs, he looks at you no matter where you go in the room. I wish he wouldn't.

"You know God's everywhere," Gerard reminds me.

"Not everywhere, Gerard. He's not in the toilet."

"Oh yes he is. He sees you going to the toilet."
"Does he? Why would he want to see that?"
"Cause he's everywhere. He just does."

MAMMY COMES UP sometimes and says a night prayer
with us,
    "O angel of God, my guardian dear
    To whom God's love commits me here
    Ever this night be at my side
    To light and guard, to rule and guide, Amen."
    When I climb into bed, I pull the clothes over
my head and hope God can't see me now. I don't
mind my guardian angel seeing me – he's nice. Or is
he a she...? Angels have skirts.

WHERE WE LIVE

Our home and shop are in Ogle Street, Armagh, on the side of the red-clay hill where St Patrick set up his church in Ireland. The High King Brian Boru is buried at the top of our hill. I don't know history, but my breath changes when I see the huge, dark-grey, grumpy cathedral up there and the ghostly Green Lady's haunted house in the terraces beneath it. Her windows are stained and filthy. I wouldn't go near there at night-time.

Below the cathedral a patchwork of slate roofs, cluttered back yards, strips of garden and makeshift clothes-lines spreads over our side of the hill, all tidied in by four streets and the Market Square. Thomas Street and Ogle Street are called after Thomas Ogle who built them. Irish Street climbs up to the Protestant Cathedral and Castle Street arcs soberly in Armagh stone around it. Chapel Lane cuts up through the middle of this patchwork, a crooked back street. We have to go quarter way up Chapel Lane to get home – we have no front door because of our shop. Our back door isn't even in Chapel Lane. It's through a shabby entry with stains on the walls where drunk men pee in the dark. Women tell my mother, "Oh, Missus Quinn, I wouldn't go up your back at night for all the tea in China!"

People stoop coming in the low back door to a ceiling that is only six and a half foot high. I like where we live, shouldered in tight to other people's backyards and the long, high stone wall of St Malachy's School. Through the day the boys there chant out sing-song spellings, sing-song tables and sing-song Hail Marys.

Armagh is a small market town of about ten thousand people. My aunt Sara says she used to walk twelve miles from Balleer into town and back every Tuesday to sell a basket of eggs and some home-made butter in front of the Market House. Rude men annoyed her when they dipped their dirty thumbs into the butter and sucked them.

Across from our shop aproned women scrub the stone step at their doors and wash their squares of footpath with a half-moon arc of wet that you're not allowed to walk on. They huddle together for muttered talk that I'd love to listen to. A few doors up, Sandy McPherson heads out to sell the stacked vegetables off his donkey and cart. I tell my sisters I'll be a 'prune man' when I grow up, with a horse and cart delivering sultanas and prunes to the people of Armagh, and I'll eat all I want. When my sister Brenda annoys me I tell her I won't be giving her any prunes.

Farmers drive cows through the streets to the Shambles Yard. The cows rebel, slowing, switching places, pissing, splashing their loose cow's clap into the street. I stop and stare at them.

Motor cars are scarce, but horses clomp up the street pulling loaded carts. The drivers sit weary, cloth-capped, on the front boards, a nod of the head or a lift of the eyebrows recognising people they know. They ease their boredom with an occasional snort of a sniff and a sideways spit. Daddy gives me a bucket and pays me a few pennies to collect steaming horse dung from the street. It's to put manure on the vegetables that mammy grows to add to the war rations.

On our own side of the street there are two coopers' shops, Tom Hill's and his brother's. Tom has a back door into our shop yard and slips in to give me a liquorice all-sort from his dungaree pocket and find out from my daddy what tips he has for the horses. He lives with his sister Teeny. Teeny smiles when she sees us, but she never comes in because they're Plymouth Brethren and she doesn't mix with Catholics. Tom doesn't seem to mind.

We live above the back of a long shop. I mustn't go up the stairs at the front, but I do. I creak up the carpeted steps when the shop is closed, through the room with the ladies' coats and dresses, and up a rickety flight to the attic. I see tea-chests full of forgotten long-ago stuff, old bills, weird gas-masks for the war, a stopped-stiff spider praying that I can't see it. I crush it with an envelope and examine its crooked legs mashed into the blood on the side of the tea-chest.

The attic is sad. Long, silent cobwebs drift up and down like waving ghosts. There's a postage stamp with a king's head on it stuck on to one of the bills. The king has a moustache and a stern face looking out to the left. If I could find a 'penny black' with Queen Victoria on it I'd be rich. Pat says it's worth fifty pounds. I search through crumpled piles of shop papers. If I could only find one 'penny black'! I'd be happy with just one.

In the evenings bad boys sit on the high school wall above our back yard. We aren't to talk to them when they shout down to us because mammy says they're bold and have no manners. We aren't to play with boys in the street either because they're bad company. We're not allowed to play in the street at all.

Our play area is the walled flat roof over our shop. Here mammy waters the pots of busy-lizzies and geraniums with cold tea. People tell her, "Oh, Missus Quinn, you've the quare green fingers!"

Her face is pink with pleasure and an edge of fluster: I think she's trying not to look proud.

She has planted sweet-pea and wall-flowers in dirt crushed with concrete blocks up against a whitewashed wall. I'm allowed to water them. I drench the dirt, punishing hidden slaters by making them flee, panicked, up the wall, a black army of refugees scurrying over the whitewash.

The view from the flat roof is of slates and Reilly's wall and the top of Parker's tree and jittery crows pecking at chimneys, though there couldn't be crumbs up there. Sometimes a great flock of birds screeches across the sky into Parker's tree. When I throw a stone, they scrawk and flutter and fly off. I'll get beat if I'm seen.

From left: Michael, Victor and Eugene on the flat roof, about 1946

Victor, Eugene and me play with a headless rocking-horse, with empty thread spools and with match-boxes filled with buttons. We feed an old wet cloth into the wooden lips of a clothes mangle and watch little streams of dirty water weeping down onto the iron frame. We throw stones at cats that dare to climb on our wall, we hunt wasps and bumble bees with upside-down milk bottles, and we count the dead flies that we squash with newspapers. We feed some, still buzzing, into a spider's web to watch the spider elbowing its way down to grab them into a death hug.

You mustn't make noise. Mammy works at the front of the shop but daddy dwells under us at the back. He squats on a bench with thread and needle, or sits on a tea-chest pedalling a sewing machine, or bangs a heavy solid iron onto a steaming cloth spread out over altered trousers. Tailor Mick. He works as hard as a flustered ant in a disturbed nest, hustling to rescue his children to the safety of 'egucation.'

I throw a stone at a crow on Reilly's roof. The crow flaps and flutters off to another chimney while the stone dances on slates as it clatters down to the spout.

Reilly opens his sky-light and puts his head out.

"Who's throwing stones?" he barks. That shout rouses daddy who bursts out of his tailor's den and surges up the wooden steps, whimpering rage as he tears off his jacket with arms and sleeves flailing like a spider. He fumbles furiously at the buckle to whip off his belt and beat me.

"Now will you throw stones at Reilly's roof!" he roars again and again as he whips me. He's making sure Reilly hears. His sputtering fury scares me more than the sharp pain welting my legs. Though that's what bold children deserve. And it's what the neighbours expect.

That is how our maids deal with boldness too, especially Ivy. She is a black shadow in the house, cramming me with fear. I am at her moody, whim-ful mercy, the oldest of the three boys and the one who should know better when we do wrong. I am the ringleader of badness in the house. A bold boy. The black sheep of the family.

"I never met the like a' you," she says, "for tellin' lies without blinkin'. You've been kep' away from the bad boys in the street but still turned out bad. God'll have it in for you, boy, when you die. He sees through your lies. You don't fool him. Nor you don't fool me!"

I wish my older sisters were around now, but all three are boarding at Middleton Convent Primary School: "The nuns give you a far better education," mammy says.

Me being bad upsets mammy. And us bickering. A few times, she is so bothered with the lot of us that she starts crying and says, "Where's my coat, I'm goin' to leave, I'm not goin' to stay any longer in this house an' be upset." I cling onto her skirt and legs and say "Please don't go. I'll try to be good." One night I dream that she's dead and I wake up crying. I can't help being bad.

I AM AWED by John Cassidy. For hours every day he stands guard on Ogle Street from his doorway next to ours. Untidy strands of dirty, long, wavy hair hang about his ears. His thick lenses are streaked with smears. His bagged trouser knees and buttoned waistcoat are grimed with tea and crumbs and with a constant dribble from his nose. Does he not notice the snotter dangling and bobbing till it breaks off? He gerns when he talks.

"Young Quinn."

"Hello, John."

"Stay out o' my garden, son."

"I wasn't in it."

"Well, somebody was. You make sure you stay out of it."

His garden is full of nettles. What is he talking about?

"I think daddy fixed your fence – it was falling over on our side."

"Awwwwh now... Who diya think made it fall over...? And that dinner your mammy gave me Sunday was cold... You tell her."

Mammy feels a pity for him and often gives him dinner.

"Okay, John. I'll be seein' you."

I go into our baby-shop next door, but he follows me in.

Helen Brennan frowns a frightened stare at him from behind the counter:

"John... What is it?"

"Be careful goin' up that street. A woman got knocked down this mornin' by a bicycle."

"Was she hurt?"

"Not too bad now – she was lucky. Just be careful."

Helen advances from behind the counter and opens the door.

"Well, thanks for tellin' us, John. I'll be careful."

John shuffles out. Helen sprays a mist of fly-killer up to the ceiling. The air fills with a choking disinfectant smell.

ALL DAY the electric men have been whistling and singing up and down the stairs. One of them keeps crooning, "Underneath the lamplight by the barricade..." (pause) "...my own Lily Marlene." No other words.

"How do you whistle," I ask the youngest man. He rounds his lips:

"Rind your lips like this, young fella, and jis' blow."

"It doesn't work for me."

"Jis' keep practisin'. It'll come."

By evening I can make a bleak, colourless sound like a ghostly wheeze through a pipe.

By then, though, something better than whistling rivets me: electric! No more torn gas mantles spluttering throaty gasps of flame. I click down a switch and make light. I click it up and make dark. Down, up, down, up, down, up, fast, making the light flash.

"Stop that," Ivy barks, "You'll waste all the electric! Keep them hands a' yours away from it. Always into mischief!"

HANRATTY'S TWO DOORS UP from our shop has a plaque on the wall telling the street that this is the house where Saint Malachy, Archbishop of Armagh, was born. I know nothing about Saint Malachy but I'm proud about it. My brother Victor is called Victor Malachy. I wish I was Michael Malachy, but they didn't give me any second name. They must have been busy.

Round the corner, in Irish Street, the church is called Saint Malachy's. Catholics like us go there. Catholics are wrinklier than Protestants and their hair isn't as smooth, but we're lucky we've got God. Protestants don't go to Mass nor nothing. They're going to get a gunk when they die and find out who was right all along. I imagine their faces. Mr Parker stands at the door of his Protestant drapery a few doors down and looks grumpy. If he knew what was coming he'd be grumpier. He never speaks to us, even looks away when we pass. Tom Hill, though, is a friendly Protestant. I'm sort of glad Mr Parker is going to hell but I feel sorry for Tom. I wish somebody would convert him, but I think they only convert black babies.

Saying, "God!" or "Christ!" or "damn" or "feckin'" is cursing and swearing. There's an even worse word, but I'm not going to write it. Sometimes daddy says "damn" when he's cross, but mammy never curses, and we don't either. Bad boys out in the street curse.

We say the Rosary at night after tea. Not most nights, only when mammy hears a sermon reminding her how important it is. Everybody kneels over a chair, and groans the back-and-forward "Heyyyyl Mary... Hooooehly Mary..." My day-dreams fill the boredom.

On Saturday evenings we have a bath, polish our shoes and put out good clothes for Mass in the morning. We go to Saint Malachy's. It's a still, soft church, full of hush, warmed by flickering candle-light and holy statues, safe and soothing in the half-dark.

A few old people whisper their prayers into the quiet, especially 'Jesus' with hissy esses. The priest makes hissy noises too at Communion time, saying 'Corpus Christi.' It's like the wiss-wiss hiss mammy used to make when she wanted me to pee in the potty. Thinking in a church about peeing in a potty is a bad thought and a sin. I wish they didn't hiss here.

Religion is sad. All round the walls are the Stations of the Cross, with small statues of Roman soldiers and sorrowful women. We mustn't get too happy. You see, Jesus is still suffering. People look sad and holy as they walk round making the Stations. I better be sad too.

MAGIC IS MY FAVOURITE THING. I'd love to be a magician like the man who came to our nursery school. I day-dream that I do magic with a stolen magic wand. Everyone is flabbergasted and wonders how I do it, but I smile and won't tell.

Santa Claus is magic. Other people wonder how he gets down sooty, narrow chimneys. Not me. If you're magic you can come through the wall. I believe in him: I don't ask questions. I don't know how Santa does it, and I don't care, he just fills me with warm love.

Priests in robes do magic too. They can turn wine into blood and they wave their hands around and say Latin things and they forgive sins.

Fairies are magic, doing bad or good with it. They do bad things if you cut down a fairy hawthorn tree in the middle of a field. Bob Corr, the Ogle Street butcher, cut down a fairy tree on his farm and his daughter took sick and there was no cure for her, and then he got a heart attack. I wonder did he not know about cutting down the tree?

God is completely magic. Like the fairies, he can do anything he likes, good or bad. He does the worst things to the ones that don't believe in him. I'm okay, I believe in him, but I hear tell of people that don't, and they are in for it unless they make a good confession before they die. There are rules you mustn't break or you're asking God for trouble. If you cut down a fairy tree, you annoy the fairies, but if you miss Mass on a Sunday, you annoy God. That's worse. It blackens your soul and you'll be in hell for ever. Mortal sins do that to you, but not venial sins like stealing less than five pounds – unless you take them off somebody that's poor. I like knowing the rules. I definitely wouldn't steal five pounds off somebody poor.

Saint Patrick's Day gives you some of the same magic feelings as Christmas. March the seventeenth is a magic date. I feel a thrill walking up Ogle Street the evening before, the coloured triangles of bunting waving at me, promising a day of bustling crowds and glorious bands. Irish tricolours flap happily from the top windows of most of the houses and I breathe in the pride of being Irish. This is our day.

We're lucky to be the friendliest, bravest country in the world that everybody loves, especially the Americans. I could cry thinking of how popular we are. God loves us that much that he turned the snakes into eels and promised St Patrick that Ireland will be covered up by the sea seven years before the end of the world. He wants to spare us the fright and misery other countries will have. I hope I'll be dead before the sea floods in.

We can't put a tricolour out the top window of our shop because some of our customers are Protestants, so mammy puts out a yellow Papal flag with the keys of Peter on it. It's just as good, she says, and doesn't offend anybody. Mrs Pettigrew is a Protestant and says mammy wouldn't offend a soul.

Protestants have their day on the twelfth of July. There's no magic about their day. A chill shivers through me thinking about it, but it's a date you don't forget. For months before the twelfth I listen to the 'batteries' rattling out hate into the sky over Armagh, and I feel afraid.

When the twelfth comes, it is their day to toot and thump. I hope the rain will drench them and I'm glad when God lets them march soaked and bedraggled. I stand on the footpath and sneak looks through the crowd at the bands and banners. Sometimes I can feel the Protestant pride churning up with the power of the big drums and the cocksure tunes. Marching their 'no' to us. They don't like Catholics and hate us feeling Irish, so we don't mention it when they're about. They look different to us. Sour, bigoted, with hard, round bowler hats. The only thing worse than them is the man in Navan Street who's a Communist.

Protestants rule Northern Ireland and they own the British army and the unfriendly police. They own the rich centre of the town, the big shops like Lennoxes and Walkers. They own English Street and Scotch Street and Market Street and the Mall where they only allow English games to be played. They think Catholics are dirty, that we keep coal in the bath and don't care about things. Catholics have to go to England to get houses and jobs. I feel spite for the word 'Protestant' and the way they treat us. But the Nationalist Party stands up for us. Senator Lennon won't let them crow over Catholics.

The IRA stands up for us too. My parents don't support them, but I'm glad when the IRA sets off bombs. I imagine having a gun. I climb down into a secret hiding place in the mountains, pull a grass roof over my head and watch through a peep-hole, waiting in the dark for the B Specials. They'll not know where the bullets come from. I'll take my revenge down here in the dark.

I LIVE HERE, off this backstreet, on our tucked-in Armagh hill, as snug as a snail in a shell. I am ruled by cross grown-ups but sheltered and soothed by mammy being close by. I'm a bold boy, but at least I'm a Catholic and we're on the right side of God. Wouldn't it be awful to be born a Protestant!

OFF TO GREENPARK

I go to school when I'm three and three quarters. Not to St Malachy's next door. Mammy says the Christian Brothers' school at Greenpark is better. She's busy, so Ivy takes me. We pass the stink of the Dips where the bin lorries dump Armagh's rubbish. Past tidy Arthur's Villas on our left, in through the green gates, down an avenue with hushed pine-trees, under an archway and into a playground echoing with boys' squeals. Ivy steps around a game of marbles, leads me into Brother Sullivan's class and over to his high desk. He has four gentle eyes through his glasses, a kind face, an old voice.

"How many noses have you?"

"Two."

"You have two nostrils," he says, twinkling at my mistake, "Just one nose."

My first question at school, and I'm wrong. I learn the word 'nostril' and hope he'll ask me again.

He gives me my place near the back of the room in an iron-framed double desk with a worn, knife-marked top and two empty inkwells. I sit quiet, my shoulder bones tight, taken out of all I know, three and three quarters, unsure of what's next. I am surrounded by boys in pullovers and short pants but glad to be separated for a while from my wee brother

Victor. I wonder if a bird will cross the square of sky I see through the high window. I hope nobody can sing as well as me.

After some weeks I walk home from school with my friend, Brian Black.

"That's good," Mammy says, "he doesn't mix with the bad boys, and I think his daddy's a policeman."

Policemen are scary, like God. They can't see you when you're on your own the way God can, but they're just as interested in finding you out doing bad things.

I like having a friend, but I don't like when mammy says he can come for my birthday. What will I do with him? Our house is boring. I'm boring.

He brings me a lucky bag with a balloon and a whistle in it. The next day, Ivy takes the whistle off me because of the noise, but the balloon is full of quiet, yellow floating. It bursts. I cry, and big brother Pat cheers me by showing me how to suck the burst skin into tiny balloon bubbles. I take a piece to school to show off what I can do.

I WALK TO SCHOOL ON MY OWN NOW, edging my way past dogs and Diggy Lug, the town madman with the starey eyes and see-saw walk. The bad boys slouch see-saw behind him and shout, "Diggy-Lug!" He turns, eyes firey, "I'll dig your lug!" The boys bend over laughing.

I gawk at huge horses outside Callaghan the Blacksmith's forge. I hop up and down on the stone step in front of Truddens Guest House (only rich people stay there, I think). I check how far I can go without walking on cracks in the footpath. I manage to skip the whole way to Greenpark without touching a crack. I stare, disgusted, at birds swirling over the mouldy rubbish in the Dips, pecking, gobbling bits, jittery, jumpy. I climb on the broken wall of the Dips and get stung on nettles, and I gut dockins onto the stings, chanting, "Dockin, dockin, in and out, take the sting of a nettle out." It still stings. I race an old man on a bicycle promising myself that mammy loves me the most if I reach the telegraph pole before him.

I like being at school now. I am stepping onto new land, still cautious, like a nervy crow near bread-crusts dropped on the footpath.

SOMETIMES I DO BAD-BOY THINGS. A horse and cart passes. Bad boys cling on to the back of the cart, lift both legs in the air and hang. Nervous, I join them, curled like a bee into the throat of a wall flower.

"Get off!" the driver shouts. I drop off, giggling and scared. The bad boys hold on a while longer until he whisks the whip at them. They drop down but shout boasts at him, "We're not afraid of you, mister! Haw-haw!"

"He better watch out," one brags, "Or I'll brak his snotter on him!"

Their roughness shocks me, but they're only bad on the outside. I'm bad on the inside. I can't help telling lies. I'd like to have my own zoo and I tell the boys at school,

"I have a zoo at home and a big lion."

Eamonn McBride challenges, "No, you don't."

"Yes, I do – you can come to our house and see." He comes to the back door, but I tell him, "You can't come in. The lion's asleep."

I LIKE HELPING, giving surprises, making breakfast for mammy and bringing it up to her, tea spilling on the stairs.

"Michael would take the sweet out of his mouth and give it to you," she says. It's true. I am generous.

Brother Sullivan asks for money for the African black babies. He collects it in the afternoon in a box with a black baby on top that nods a sad smile at you when you put money in. He slices an apple among the boys who have a penny or a ha'penny to give, cutting the apple with a penknife into thick, delicious slices.

I want to help the black babies. I want to hear the clink and jingle of my penny in the box. Most of all I want Brother Sullivan to notice me being generous.

I have to find more pennies. The wooden till in our shop is full of money. I better not be seen. I tip-toe down the wooden steps early before school. I slide open and closed the back door into the shop, wincing at each creak. In front of the till I slide out the drawer so slowly. My chest thumps out thuds of risk and wrong-doing. I see pennies, sixpenny bits, shillings, half-crowns, a thrilling spread of money in each section. It is as scary as my body can bear to ease out the top penny into my fingers and press the drawer quietly, softly back.

Once into the street I hum a tune as if this is an ordinary day. I can't wait for Brother Sullivan's smile at my goodness.

I visit the till often after that.

"THE WAR IS OVER," Pat tells me, "Hitler's dead."

"Is he...? Are you glad he's dead?"

"Course I am. Everybody's glad."

"Then so am I glad too."

Hitler's a baddie with black hair and a moustache. We're on rations because of him. A family is only allowed a quarter pound of sweets in a week and a packet of tea and a small bag of sugar and not much butter. We get home-made butter from our aunties in the country and we smuggle things in from the free state.

Smuggling is okay, everybody smuggles, even me. One day we're coming home in the train and they give me a packet of tea to stuff up my pullover.

"No, not up the front where it'll stick out. Up the side. Stuff it up the side. They'll never search a young chil' like you."

The train stops at Goraghwood. A customs officer with a hard face darkens the carriage and drones,

"Any goods to declare..."

I am in a grip of panic, in a flutter, struggling to hold back my trembles. My face must look confused and guilty. He's bound to notice... I feel his deadly presence as he stalks up, a disgruntled lion, a hawk... And he's passed! I am a prisoner freed from jail – and alive with pride that I have got one over on a Customs Officer with my packet of tea.

I AM BRAINY, Brother Sullivan says, so I skip the Senior Infants class straight into First Class and Brother O'Connor's dark classroom. I hate school. I feel the dread in the bottom of my belly from I wake up in the morning. I flounder, stupid, able at spellings and tables but stumbling at sums. For two years I don't understand where the small number comes from at the bottom of the tens and hundreds columns. Nearly always I guess it wrong. I hate the foreign language of catechism and the uncertainty of what a teacher expects.

I escape to a brighter world, a cheered hero who scores impossible goals at football. Brother O'Connor swoops.

"Quinn! Ask me a question!"

"Sir..."

I am numb. How does a nobody ask a question?

"Sir... A question?"

"I'm waiting, Quinn."

"Sir..."

He's waiting. I am keeping an adult waiting.

"Sir..."

What do I say? What question...?

"Are you going to ask me a question, Quinn?"

"Yes, sir. Sir..."

I draw in my breath to ask. I have no idea what to say. Please ask somebody else, can't you see I'm stupid!

"If you don't ask me a question fast, you'll be slapped."

My mouth saves me.

"Sir.., what's two and two?"

As soon as my mouth says it, I'm sorry. That's a stupid question. It's too late to change it.

"Good, that's a question – what's two and two? Answer – Two and two is four. A question... gets an answer. Now... Mackey, ask me a question."

"Sir, what was it like during the war?"

Oliver Mackey has brains. He doesn't need his mouth to save him. He's lucky. But this morning I got by.

NOW VICTOR HAS STARTED in Brother Sullivan's class and I have to walk to school with him, tethered again, stuck to him. Drawling, dawdling Victor, who walks with maddening won't-hurry wonder at leaves and worms and a daddy-long-legs.

"Hurry up!" I say. I correct him that a goose is not a big long duck and my sister's cello is not a big, long fiddle. He still says them wrong. One morning he breaks his leg on Trudden's steps and gets the plaster of Paris that I would love. I wish I could break my leg.

Eugene has started school now too, and the 'three boys' have to walk together. Sometimes I play with my two wee brothers, but I still hate them.

WHEN YOU'RE SEVEN you make your First Confession because you're old enough to commit sins. You have to learn your catechism and know all the words off by heart, or you won't be allowed to make it. I know all about heaven or hell if the priest asks me, or the number of persons in God. I'm even okay about limbo and purgatory. I know a good bit about mortal and venial sins but not deadly sins like sloth and lust. I'm not sure about having strange Gods before me or coveting my neighbour's wife or my neighbour's goods (Mr Toman says his goods are things like his donkey). I hope the priest doesn't ask me questions with long words in the answers like 'sanctifying grace' or 'plenary indulgences.'

A nice priest arrives with a quiff and brylcreem in his hair and a pipe that he lights three times. He's in a good mood, doesn't even ask us the questions, just chats to the Master and asks us:

"Are yiz all ready for your First Confession, boys?"

"Yeeehes, father!"

He smiles. And he passes every one of us!

A priest is never shocked by what you say in Confession. I can tell him about murder or anything. I just have to be sorry and tell him how many times. I queue on the kneeler, feeling the strangeness. 'I told lies' is easy. Telling about stealing will be harder. The embarrassing sin is that I threw our mustard holder over Reilly's low wall. I just wanted to see it fall and hear the glass smash. I go in the door to sudden darkness and a woody confession-box smell different to any other woody smells. The priest is waiting, concentrated, behind the grille.

"Father, this is my first confession. I told lies and I stole money and I threw the mustard holder over Reilly's wall."

There's a long, dark pause. The priest is wondering about the mustard-holder. I hope he doesn't ask me how much I stole. Slowly it occurs to me that I've been talking to wood. The grille is closed. There is a rattle and a slide and the head and shoulders of a priest takes shape dimly. He smells of cigarettes and more confession-box. Again I begin. He asks for no details and blesses me in Latin through the grille. I float out into the brightness of the church, wiped white, the load gone, a good boy, no more lies or stealing.

It's hard to stay good when the floating fades. I still steal. I lie. I search through mammy's magazines to see women in their underwear. And I am back to confession once a month. Father McKee is the quickest, the best, doesn't ask details. I rhyme my sins, "I told lies and I committed sins and that's all I can remember, Father." I feel cleaned afterwards, good again.

First Communion morning comes. Like a birthday. I wear the handed-down white short-pants suit that Gerard and Pat wear in the photographs on the sitting room wall. Before we leave I stand before the mirror and worship myself in striking white.

Saint Patrick's Cathedral is full of girls in white dresses and boys in long-pants blue serge suits. The gunk! I'm different. Wretchedly, childishly white among the long dark suits. My spirit collapses like the starlet that winged into our window last winter. I am frantic, desperate to be away, out of my suit, back home. It's like the day the zip of my pants was open in front of the class and I was being giggled at. Only this is far worse.

I go up to receive Jesus, mortified, smothered in shame. A priest puts the white Body of Christ on my tongue. It is too thin to be bread. It melts into mush and Jesus drops down, disappointed, into my ugly gurgling belly and my drooped soul. Poor God!

Back in my seat I am supposed to pray and be thankful. The prayer can't get started through the fluster and shame.

Now I have to fast from midnight every Saturday night because I'm going to get God into me, and God doesn't like to be mixed in with mushy, vomity food. One Sunday morning I can't believe they left the biscuit barrel open. I nip a broken one into my pocket, saunter into the lavatory and stuff it into my mouth. In Saint Malachy's, I suddenly remember, "I'm not fasting!" Fear cramps my tummy: if I don't go up to the altar rails, they'll think, "That boy must have a mortal sin on his soul that he's not takin' communion!" What can I do?

I stay in the seat when they file out for Communion. I tell them after Mass that I ate a crumb off the table. They believe me.

I'M IN MR CUSH'S CLASS now. I want to be in his Christmas operetta, to sparkle on the stage, not just flicker in the choir at the back. Mr Cush considers me. I might do as one of the three Spanish ladies.

"Try whirling yourself around, swinging your arms..?"

He doesn't say I'm awkward: I know from his face.

I tell mammy I'm going to be a Spanish Lady in the opera. Everybody knows Michael tells lies, but they believe me because I half-imagine I have the part.

As a member of the choir, I attend the practices. I dream that one of the Spanish ladies takes ill and the teacher asks me to take the part. I enjoy everyone's surprise as they watch me dance, light and lovely, across the stage, a star...

On the evening of the opera, my mother wears her fur coat, and Pat and Brenda are allowed to go with her to see me. I have little sense of a dream ending – they are here to watch me shine.

After the show Brenda punctures the dream.

"Why did you tell lies?"

"What lies? What do you mean?"

"You weren't a Spanish lady. You were just in the choir!"

"I was a Spanish lady. Did you not see me?"

"You weren't! Look, here's the programme. Here's the three Spanish ladies."

"I know I'm not in the programme. I was standing in for Garrett McCreesh - he had to go home early. Did you not see me?"

"That's a lie and you just won't admit it!"

Mammy says little. I think she's wondering what will become of me.

Later the Spanish lady becomes a family story. Mention of it brings laughter and head-shaking.

"Michael," they say, "can tell lies without blinking."

They're wrong. I am a poor liar. I attempt to cover up my stealing with lies, "Imagine. I found a ten-shilling note." Yet I redden and look guilty as I swear innocence.

My dreaming is different: the Spanish lady is more a longing than a lie.

WITH MY SEVENTH BIRTHDAY COMES a stamp-album that draws me in under a new magic spell. I am entranced, captivated by my sprouting collection of stamps, these precious little squiggle-edged paper treasures. Heads of kings and queens hold magic for me, but I am rapt at the sight of multi-coloured flowers, African wild animals, aeroplanes, my first triangle-shaped stamp! I drool over my collection as a miser might count his gold. A sort of Scrooge with my stamps.

I'M IN KIND MR TOMAN'S CLASS. You can ask him questions and he doesn't get cross. He knows what the rules are. At religion time, I ask him,

"Sir."

"What is it, Quinn?"

"Sir, supposin' a man dies... An' when they're lowerin' him down into the grave, the lid comes off the coffin... An' the dead man is inside with his mouth open. An' supposin', sir, a dog comes along just at that minute... An' it's got a bit o' meat in its mouth... An' sir, it drops the meat... An' supposin' it's a Friday, sir, when we're not allowed to eat meat, and say the meat drops down right into the dead man's mouth..."

"Stop it, Quinn. Stop...! Your imagination's running away with you!"

"But, sir, would he be committin' a sin?"

"How could a dead man commit a sin!"

"So he wouldn't..."

I didn't think it would be a sin. I'm not good at keeping the rules myself, but I like to have someone who can tell me what they are.

IT IS SPRING and I am on my own, walking to school. I have never seen the clouds so happy in the sunshine. The branches of an elm tree are stretching out fingers brimming with new-green leaves that tremble into the stillness. I tremble too... Birds singing add more magic. Is this what that poet felt about the golden daffodils? I love being part of it.

FAMILY

Babies come dropped down from God. My sister Gabe was found by Father Victor Marron at the side of the road, at a bend where he had to slow his motor-car. He gave her to mammy. The luck! She could have ended up in a gypsy caravan. Victor was found in John Cassidy's garden under the nettles, not even stung. John Cassidy never washes. Imagine if he had found Victor! I was found in the garden at number 10 Ogle Street, beside cabbages, all covered in dirt. My sister Anne found me and took me upstairs and washed me. I might have been there for weeks if she hadn't heard a wee squeak. I'm glad I wasn't dropped into somebody else's garden.

You're born with no clothes. Mammy says your bare skin is your birthday suit, but I don't like being bare. You're not supposed to let anybody see your bum or your wee-wee. Boys have wee-wees and girls have got nothing - just bums. They're called your private parts. You're not allowed to look at anybody else's or talk about them.

My sister Anne tells me she can get honey out of her breast. I tell everybody at the table what she said and they all get angry and shout at me and daddy sends me up the stairs to bed. 'Breast' is a dirty word.

MY PARENTS have nine children.

Gerard is my hero who can kill witches and knows about music and Ireland and used stamps. When he sings 'She moved through the fair' in his soft broken voice an electric thrill sizzles inside me. I'm definitely going to learn that song too. I imitate the special way he has of tossing his wavy quiff back off his forehead, but my hair's too short: it doesn't move.

"Stop shakin' your head like that," Pat warns, "or you'll end up with a twitch and you won't be able to stop."

I can ask Gerard about things.

"What would you do if you met a witch, Gerard?"

"I'd grab her by the arm and twist it behind her back an' force her down onto the ground, then I'd get a knife and stick it into her."

Easy. I know it's true: he really can kill witches.

ANNE IS SECOND: she has a sharp nose, kind, shiny eyes, and gives you the tightest hugs and kisses. A little mammy to us all. She chats away to everyone, even me. She teaches me proper manners that the nuns taught her: I should always keep to the outside of the footpath when I'm with a lady so the lady won't be splashed; I should place a turned-up fork beside a knife when I finish eating; I should hold a cup of tea with my little finger curled out politely.

How does she see through her hair! She swipes it back and seconds later it slips back round in front of her eyes. I wouldn't stick that. When she plays the fiddle, she clips the hair back, her face turns concentrated and serious, her left wrist bends up like a hump, her fingers quiver and her elbow flails as she dashes the bow up and down in strokes you can hear all over the house. The music she plays is called classical, it's not great, doesn't have much tune, but watching her playing fascinates me.

From left: Eugene, Anne, Pat, my father, Brenda, Victor, Frances (on my mother's knee), Gabrielle, Gerard and myself.

Anne is at St Louis' Boarding School in Kilkeel. One Sunday we all board Frank Toner's taxi to visit her. At the sharp bend into Markethill everyone in the packed back seat crushes against me and my elbow weighs down on the handle. Suddenly the door is open. I curl into a ball as my shoulder hits the tarmac and I barrel over and over along the road into grass and briars. The taxi has sped on. They're leaving me behind! I leap up, panicked, and run after it.

"Jesus, Mary and Joseph," Frank gasps. "A child is after fallin' out a' the car!"

My mother covers her eyes as Frank brakes. She hears running footsteps. "Mick's away to pick up the child," she thinks.

Panting, I reach the car. Just a bruise on my shoulder and patches of tar on my clothes.

"I thought yiz were goin' to go on without me," I whimper.

Such a fuss over me! I am the talk of the family and the neighbours for days. I limp a bit to invite more attention.

PAT IS NEXT. Some boys say, 'Pat the rat' to him. A rat's face is pointed but Pat's is rounder than anybody else in our family – 'rat' is a stupid name. All the same, I'm glad my name doesn't rhyme with a rat. Pat said he would give me a penny if I drank my own pee, but he never gave me the penny. Mammy says he's the top singer in the cathedral choir.

"They'd be lost without him, he sings like an angel," she says.

One day in the garden Pat calls Anne a silly bitch.

"I'm goin' to tell mammy what you said!"

"No, you're not! No, you're not!"

Pat grabs daddy's hatchet to guard the door out of the garden.

"You're not gettin' past!"

Anne pushes on. Pat swings the hatchet and clouts the blade down on her forehead. Sobered by the sight of blood, he lets her pass. Her screams alert Helen who scoops her up and dashes her off to have the cut stitched. Pat is in for it! I'm shocked: I wouldn't hit anybody with a hatchet, especially on the head.

Pat takes me fishing. We tie lengths of cord around the lips of jam jars and head for the Callan bridge. Fleets of spricks sail in and out of the shadows of stones, timid but curious. I clap my hands at them and they flee.

"Don't, Michael," Pat warns. "Now they won't come back for a while. Throw in your jar now anyway while they're gone."

We splash in the jars and watch them sink down to settle on the mud, the white tails of cord floating up towards us. We whisper as a few scouts venture back, then a full, slow fleet twisting and jerking towards the jars. I am a caveman on his first hunt. A curious sprick finds the mouth of my jar and jerks in.

"Pull, Michael, quick," Pat whispers. I heave my jar out of the water. Too late. How did it escape? We wait till they return.

Pat has a big two-pound jar and captures three panicked fish in one heave. "The bigger the jar, the better chance you have a' catchin' them."

I wish I had one of the huge glass sweetie jars out of Missus McGreevey's shop. We go home with seven fish. I caught one of them. I can't wait to tell everyone. I marvel at our captives through the glass.

GABE IS NUMBER FOUR in the family, called after Angel Gabriel, she says, the same as I'm called after Archangel Michael. Angel Gabriel was a boy-angel and Gabe wishes she was a boy. I'm surprised anybody wants to be a boy. I want to be a girl because they're lovelier and because that would give me a chance to look at where girls' pee comes out. I keep quiet about my wish.

During the war Gabe was left with our aunt Minnie to keep her safe from bombs. She was left so long that she thinks Minnie is her mammy. She's back home, pining for Minnie, and is a 'delicate child' who needs goat's milk.

BRENDA IS JUST two years older than me, at the bottom of the three girls. Her job is to look after us three boys, even bathing us together in the one bath on Saturdays. I rebel:

"Bossy, bossy, bossy! Benny beats bums! Ne-ne-ne-ne-ne!"

I'm glad, though, when Brenda shows me how to do things, how to make magic sparks in the dark coal shed by grating white flint stones against each other, how to use my thumbnail to snip the red flower off a fuschia in just the right spot to suck out honey. I suck the sweetness out of dozens and dozens of fuschia blossoms.

I'M NEXT IN THE FAMILY. No, the 'three boys' are next, Michael, Victor and Eugene. I hate being 'the three boys.' We have the same play, the same bedtimes, the same meals at the wee round table in the upstairs bedroom. Everybody else is at the big table downstairs. When it's time to come in somebody calls "Michael, Victor and Eugene," never Michael. I hate my wee brothers being stuck on to me and making me 'the three boys.'

LAST IS FRANCES, a wrapped-up baby that I'd love to hold:

"All right, one second. Now, don't drop her... Okay, that's enough."

"But I didn't drop her. I wouldn't. I wouldn't..."

WE HAVEN'T MANY VISITORS. Larry Leonard raps at the back door, holy and wheezy, collecting for the missions. He's given his money but isn't invited in.

Father Victor Marron is a far-out cousin of mammy's and he's invited for dinner with a tablecloth and the china plates because he's a priest and wrote a book, *My American Visit*. He arrives to great fuss, a big, friendly man who remembers all our names and who laughs by sniffing loud breaths up and down his huge nose. He smells like a priest – a strange talcum-powder and black-cloth smell. Right across the top of his head he has smoothed thatch-coloured threads of hair from the other side so that he won't look baldy. He likes roast beef. When he finishes eating it, he wonders, "Ciss, would you like more meat?" I think that's a polite way to ask, for she jumps up to give him another helping. I feel lucky and proud that somebody so important visits us. Not too many people have even an ordinary priest for dinner.

AUNTIE ROSE LANDS for a few days at Christmas. I pretend I'm glad, that I'm not afraid of her, and I give her a kiss.

"Och, hello, Auntie Rose, you're welcome."

She sits up close to the fire, blocking the heat from the rest of us and repeats in a cranky voice, "Would you close that door...   ...an' keep it closed!"

I'm lucky I don't have to stay in her house in Ballybay. When Brenda and Gabe stay, she doesn't allow them out the door. Worse than that, she makes them eat fat.

"It's the best part of the meat! If there's any left on your plate, I'll put it into your soup."

Auntie Rose is short and stout and her legs have wads of crinkled fat like the elephant's ankles I saw in Dublin zoo. She pokes a hand up her long skirt to footer into a pocket in her knickers, fishes out a hankie and blows a few flushes of snotters into it before sticking it back up. We giggle about her knickers when we go upstairs – but not in front of her, nor not in front of mammy or daddy. Boys are not supposed to say 'knickers,' but I like saying it.

Mammy says to go in and talk to her, she's lonely. I hope somebody else joins me for she talks family history and I don't know who the people are.

"No, Sarah Ann Duffy was a different Duffy – they came from near Keady. She might have been a sister-in law to one of the McEneaney girls, you know the ones that their father died of pneumonia... och, you do know who I'm talkin' about, do you not mind he died on Ash Wednesday just a year ago..."

Auntie Rose is the oldest of mammy's sisters, the first to go to America, the last to come home (after twenty-two years), and the only one who didn't marry. Mammy says she was beautiful and could have taken her pick of the men there. One night a man asked to leave her home from a dance and she answered, "I can go home myself!" When she's not around and we want a laugh, one of my brothers or sisters will say in a squeaky Monaghan accent, "I can go home myself!"

SOMETIMES ON SUNDAYS we visit uncles and aunts. St Christopher carried Christ safe across water, so we pray to him for a safe journey. I have a holy picture of St Christopher wading into a river with baby Jesus on his shoulders.

Mammy's sister Auntie Nell has a farm and a small country shop in Ballymacully. Nell is a tidy wee woman in an apron and farm boots. I am shocked that she doesn't even boggle at the tough, sweaty work she does outside the house. Out in the field bent over as she digs and scoops up potatoes. Tossing hay up into stacks with her pitch-fork. Tying and stooking flax and corn, even mowing grass with a scythe. Auntie Nell has a blurred eye where someone stuck a pen into it when she was a schoolgirl. She never tells me the story of it without warning me, "Now, never you stick a sharp object into somebody's eye: your eye is a very precious thing." I don't know why she tells me: I wouldn't dream of sticking something sharp into anybody's eye.

Uncle Jemmy and Auntie Nell always make us welcome. My cousin Eugene shows me how to spy on birds: we find a thrush's nest and take turns to gaze at the treasure of spotted blue eggs in her delicate wee shelter. How can a bird build this elegant little den with only a beak and a claw? Eugene says,

"Come away now or the mammy might get nervous and not come back."

UNCLE JOHN lives in Balleer, Tassagh, where daddy was born. His eyes sparkle at us.

"What age are you now, Michael... And who's teachin' you..? Is he any good of a teacher...?"

His dark eyebrows jump up and down as he listens. His widening eyes treat my answers like startling news.

"Oh, my, my!" he says, "Man dear. Is that so? Well, that's a terra'! Oh-my-oh-my-oh-my!"

His children show us how to snare rabbits and whistle at sheep-dogs. I'm proud of Uncle John – they say he's the best trainer of collie sheep dogs in County Armagh. I love him when he slips a half-crown real quiet into my hand before we leave.

DADDY BRINGS US TO LISADIAN where his sister Sara is married to Uncle Davey Conlon. Sara is a bright, small, red-haired woman with a worried face and a pointy chin like mine. She was eight when her mammy died and she hasn't stopped working since, alert at school yet half-rearing my daddy and his wee brother, John, dishing up meals, feeding hens and calves, later sewing up waistcoats for daddy at ten bob a time – and still taking time to pray for everybody.

Davey is her match at working, a tall, wiry man with a brave shock of hair and gnarled, leathery hands: he worked in a quarry from six to six every day and a half-day Saturdays to save money and buy his farm. His children are all ferocious workers, farming before and after school and constantly hefting buckets brimming with water from the well. Davey's eyes shine with fun when we turn up:

"Go for them, childer, wrestle them to the groun', they're on'y soft town childer!"

His boys charge and floor us, and we surrender, laughing. Off we go together then to roll our boiled Easter eggs down a sloped field. The shells won't crack, so we fling the eggs up to smash them: they splatter scraps of yoke and white across the grass. We poke lumps out of the shells, but I miss salt and pepper. Auntie Sara then sits us in to her kitchen to new-baked scones and jam, and milk straight from real cows.

Out we charge after that to look for the nests of clocking hens in the hedges. Victor is praised for rousing a mammy hen and finding nine eggs in a nook. I wish I could have found them.

I STAY A WEEK with daddy's uncle and aunt in Seagahan, Mick and Mary Anne McKee. They are the oldest people I know. When Uncle Mick seems to be dozing, I nab his round-handled walking stick, crouch over it, humped, then hobble and shuffle my way across the floor to see what it feels like to be old. He wakes up and smiles, "Mockin's catchin'!"

Neighbours turn up now and again for his cure of the sprain. Uncle Mick won't take money, so they leave him potatoes or a bag of apples. Before he dies, he says, he'll pass on the cure to somebody. I hope he gives it to me – I'd like to do magic.

Uncle John comes in his pony and trap on Sundays to take them to Mass in Ballymacnab church.

"He's always early for us or there wouldn't be any places left at the church to tie his pony."

I squeeze in beside Auntie Mary Anne in the neat wooden seat of the trap with its soft leather backing. The speed, the jangle and the clap-clap trot of the pony is far better fun than a ride in Frank Toner's taxi.

FRANK TONER DROPS US OFF in Billeady to visit mammy's sister Auntie Minnie at the old family home. A pile of dung is alive with flies as we pass up the yard. Minnie opens her half-door and comes fussing out, hopping from one foot to another, gobsmacked, her arms shaking like a jerky fiddle bow:
"Ah! Ah now! A wonder yiz wouldn't of let me know yiz were comin'! I'd of killed a chicken for yiz and made scowns. Ah Gawd!"
Auntie Minnie is a wee wrinkled woman with a pinched, caring face, wirey hair, two soft, mousey eyes like the tiny beads of a rosary, a few long hairs curling out of her chin, a thin body worn out with goodness. She's not long back from Mass, still wearing her Sunday best – a long black coat and a hat with a sprig of imitation berries pinned onto the side of it. She takes off the coat, ties a potato sack in front of her dress and spoons tea leaves into a kettle.
"An' yiz come with not a word a' notice. Ah, dear, what were yiz thinkin' at all!"
I am shocked that she's wearing a pair of men's boots and thick, puckered stockings on her spindly legs. I'd be ashamed to live here. Minnie looks poor and old-fashioned, the beds smell musty and I might get diseases from the dirt. A bucket of water from the well sits on her cracked floor. There's no stove, only creaky black irons to swing back over an open fire and bake griddle bread or boil potatoes in a black pot. The

tea-kettle is wheezing above the flames. Three hens wander into the kitchen after us and she shoos them out.

"Drat them hens!"

I blow the bellows to watch the flames flare up, but mammy tells me not to be burning up all her turf. There's nothing left to do.

Auntie Minnie can't read or write because she stayed at home to look after my granny. Her quaint clothes and funny talk, even the country way she walks all put me off. I know she is all generosity and gives you whatever she has – but I don't want it. She hands me strong tea in a chipped mug. I'd rather not drink out of it, but she might be upset if I don't.

Above: a 'meitheal' of local people gathered for a day to pull flax on my aunt Minnie's farm in Billeady in the 1920s. They generally felt well rewarded with plenty of food, mugs of tea and meeting up again.

ONE DAY I AM IN THE ROOM OVER THE SHOP. I don't know why I feel so miserable, so wretched. I don't know why I'm crying. I crawl behind the couch and sob, scrunched in where nobody opening the door will see me. On my tongue I catch tears and lick the salty tracks. My sobbing comes back in heaves.

Gerard comes in. I stop crying, waiting for him to go away, but he has heard me.

"Michael?"

"What?"

"Where are you? What's wrong? Come on out."

His voice is kind. Reluctantly, slowly, I creep out.

"What is it? What's wrong?"

Tears and snot smear my face. I feel ugly.

"Nobody cares about me!" I slobber, "Nobody here likes me."

Tears leak from my eyes and nose and then burst.

Gradually, the sobs slow, and my eyes blink through the tears at my brother. He is lovely beside me, noticing me, angry for me.

He speaks to mammy about me being 'neglected.' I've heard that word before, but it sounds new and important. Am I a neglected child?

MY PARENTS

You're supposed to love Jesus more than everybody else. I don't. I love mammy the most. I don't feel any love for Jesus at all, but I say "I love you" to him anyway because he's powerful and can keep you out of heaven.

You have to love your mammy and daddy the same. When people ask, "Who do you love the most, your mammy or your daddy?" I always lie, "Both the same." There's no comparison. Daddy is jaggy to kiss and bony, he's rough when he plays tigers with us under the table, and he always finds a job for me when he sees me – thread needles, rinse his ironing cloth, rip the thread off trouser bottoms, darn socks, sew on buttons with a thimble, dry the dishes, gather up weeds he has dug in the garden and shake the clay off them...

I'm not sure, but I don't think mammy loves daddy as much as daddy loves her. She's glad of him, I think, but she's better educated and knows she can talk to anybody. Daddy talks easy to country people and farmers but he likes it when mammy takes over the talk with visitors. She loves telling stories and adds bits that never happened. I'm not supposed to interrupt and tell her she's wrong because interrupting is bold. She interrupts daddy and takes over telling his story. I think he's relieved to have the story taken off him. So am I. She's is better at telling things.

Daddy's name is Arthur Michael, called after his daddy, Arthur. Everybody calls him Mick – or Tailor Mick. He was born on the seventh of May 1899 in Balleer, Tassagh, Co. Armagh. He reads slow and not much – a prayer book and the page about horses at the back of the Irish News. He writes even less – just his own name and the names of horses. Anne tells me he was only six when his mammy died, and he wasn't interested in school any more. At the Balleer school, the principal saw that he loved to be outside and often had him rooting away at his garden instead of learning with the rest of the class. Daddy deems he has missed out on 'egucation' and has his mind set on none of us making that mistake. He works fixed, relentless, to put money aside for us and our schooling.

I nearly always know what he's going to say. When he plays draughts with me, it isn't long till he announces, "Position is everything in life." When he doesn't think much of something, he'll say, "That's as I roved out." When he likes a story, the eyes glisten, he sticks out his closed lips and sighs, "Aah!" or, "I houl' you." When he sees me slouching, he straightens up and says, "Head up, chin in, back straight!" Right enough, he keeps his own chin in and back straight.

If I make a mistake, he'll say, "I cautioned you, but you don't listen." It's bad enough when a drop of ink falls on my homework without him advising, "You should never drop ink on the page!" He makes up a new rule as soon as I do something wrong – "You should never go too close to a Christmas tree!" when I accidentally knock a decoration off the tree!

Daddy takes me cycling the odd Sunday morning and drifts out towards Tassagh where he grew up.

"This wee village is Milford, just a row a' houses. An' tha's the shoe factory. Thon's Knipe's field– the one wi' the gap in the hedge up near the top 'a the hill. And over there, look, there's McKeever's barn. She's a widda woman lives in there with a son that's not right... dunno what happened him, might a' bin born that way…"

I sense he loves telling me this stuff, loves the company, hungers for it, but his lore bores me into silence.

Now and again he takes me walking to watch men playing bullets on the Rock Road. Groups huddle around. Nothing is happening.

"Will we go, daddy, I'm freezin'!"

"Whisht, it'll start now in a minit."

A man takes off his jacket and rolls up the shirt sleeves. He weighs a cannon-ball in his hand, steps back, further back, then rushes at the chalked line, his right arm rigid as a stick behind his back. Near the line he stoops low to swing the arm down and shoot the bullet off. It boulders itself along with those special metal-on-rock bouncing thuds, then settles into a distinct rumbling roll. Ke-hohs of cheer rise up, then shouts of alert far down the road to clear people out of the bullet's track.

Another day daddy and I are on the road when shouts echo out and a cannon-ball hurtles down towards us. What would happen if I stopped it? I don't dare: I'd be more afraid of the men's anger – and daddy's – than of hurting my leg.

CLOTH IS RATIONED. Daddy needs it to make suits. He smuggles a load of suit-lengths across the Monaghan border and stores them under the hay on auntie Margaret's farm in Derrynoose. Every Wednesday, when the shops are closed for the half-day, he cycles up through Keady to bring some home on the carrier of his bike. One day a customs officer steps out in front of him.

"Where did this cloth come from?"

"Ehhh... I... I don't know..." daddy flusters.

"We've been watching you, Mr Quinn. We know what you're up to. You better tell us all about it."

The story comes out in pieces and the cloth is traced back to the dump in Derrynoose. In the court case daddy is fined three hundred pounds or six months in jail. He decides three hundred is too much: they send him to Crumlin Jail in Belfast. His time there isn't too bad – the wardens are glad of a tailor to mend their own clothes. He never talks to us about his time there.

The men's department at the back of the shop is where daddy rules. Two men, Paddy Curry and Billy Irwin, help with the sewing. Before he goes out the door, Paddy clicks his heels like an American soldier, salutes me and says, 'Addy-Oats, ameego' (that's

Spanish for Cheerio, he says). Billy is always trying to shock: his neighbours are mad with him because he calls his dog 'Jingle-bollocks,' but I like the sound of it. He tells me we all come from monkeys, but I'm not that easy fooled – he must think I would believe anything because I'm small!

DADDY DOES THE MONEY. He has sewed an extra money pocket into the front of his trousers and fixed a button on it. When he needs change of a fiver, he turns from a customer, searches down into the pocket and pulls out a fat roll of pound notes tied with a rubber band he has sliced off a bicycle tube. There must be fifty pounds there. So much money flabbergasts me.

He takes me across the border to Dundalk to put money in the post office where the taxman won't be able to get it off him.

"This'll be your money someday. When you're twenty-one. There'll be a few hundred for each of you. It'll start yiz off."

A fat woman in the post office has a puckered face and thick glasses. Her grey hair is wrapped into a hair-net, but I can see a patch where she's going baldy. I try not to stare at it. I think she has worries. Daddy hokes into the money pocket, moves in close to the counter and hands across his post office book and five wads of white fivers. The woman counts them out at speed, only stopping to wet her thumb with her tongue.

"Two hundred and fifty pounds."

She dips a pen into a bottle of ink, writes into daddy's book and spreads a blotter over the ink.

"What's the interest now?"

"Two an' a half percent."

"I see. Thanks now."

As he leaves, Daddy clears his throat like, "I'm not a bit nervous in here." I think he is. Outside, he warns me, "Now you know what to say if anybody asks you, *Where were you? – Don't know. What were you doin'? – Don't know.*"

We slink away. You never know who might be watching us and wondering what's that pair doing in a post office in Dundalk.

DADDY UPSETS CHRISTMAS DAY. I don't think he feels the magic. The shop is closed and he can't work. He brushes and tidies the yard. There's nothing left to work at after dinner. Pat says something wrong and there is a flare of temper. Daddy right-fists the low ceiling and, his knuckles bleeding, pushes Pat outside the back door. I cry with fright and mammy whimpers about her bad nerves. She says Christmas is spoilt.

Next day is Boxing Day. The shops are closed, but we have to work. Daddy smashes down a wall with a sledge hammer to make the shop longer, and he organises us to bucket rubble through the shop, across the street and into Corvin's Meadow at the back of the baby shop. I want to play with my new toys. I can't bear this bucket handle biting into my fingers. The decorations in the shop don't dance any more: there's just a whispering sigh from the floating paper trapped in sellotape.

Everybody else says they had a quiet Christmas. Daddy tells people he had a quiet Christmas too. Not for us. He burst the swelled yellow balloon of Christmas into flat scraps.

DADDY TEACHES US anything he knows. I stay out of his track.

He shows me how to use a saw when I'm eight. He pencils a line across a plank of wood and hoists the plank onto an old chair.

"You put your knee on the plank and you grip a tight hold of it before you start to cut. You can't be too careful..."

"Okay. Let me have a go..."

"Whisht... You keep your eye on the line and you cut with the heel a' the saw, watch..."

The saw fumbles a few seconds and then rasps into the plank.

"Ach, daddy, you're doin' it. Are you not goin' to let me?"

"Listen! Are you watchin'? Heel! Heel! Heel! You go into it with the heel."

"I know, daddy. Will you not let me? You've nearly got it all cut. I thought I was going to cut it."

"That'll do you! No back-talk! Now, take the saw... Cut... Steady... Naw, give it the heel, give it the heel. Here, give me it, you're not givin' it the heel!"

He takes the saw and lets it grind down and back into the screeching plank.

"Och, you've done it all. How do you expect me to learn if you won't let me do it myself!"

"Watch yourself, boy! I'll crig you if I hear one more bit a' back-talk out a' you. Now put away the saw, and watch how you hold it. Like this – no, in tight like so, or you'll do yourself damage. Careful..."

I go off cross.

Now he wants me to take a parcel to Mrs Corvin's on Cathedral Row. Okay if he would just let me go.

"Go the back road, over the hill. If you meet anybody, you don't talk to them unless they talk to you first. If they ask you *What's in the parcel? –* you've on'y one answer, *Don't know."*

"Okay!"

"If they ask you, *Where are you goin'? – Don't know*! *Who sent you? – Don't know. What's your name? Don't know."*

"Och daddy, I couldn't say that..."

"Are you goin' to take the parcel or are you not? Do I have to take it myself?"

"Okay, I'll take it."

Mrs Corvin lives in a swanky house in Cathedral Row. She is a far-out relation and asks me in for a glass of lemonade.

"Here you are, love. Go inside to the sitting room, there's a plate of cakes in there."

Why does she call buns 'cakes'? It doesn't stop me eating them. I never get buns like this – in wee crinkly bun wraps with caps of pink and yellow icing smothering over them, some of them crowned with a cherry. There are seven on a china plate. Mammy always says to clean your plate, not to leave scraps. I'm on my fifth bun when Mrs Corvin gives a cup of tea to a new visitor and tells her, "There's a plate of cakes inside. I'll be in after you in a moment."

I'm glad I didn't eat the last two.

DADDY EMBARRASSES ME. He sends me to Paddy McKee for a haircut and he gives me sixpence.

"But it's ninepence for a haircut, daddy."

"Tell him that's all your daddy would give you."

After the haircut, I tell Paddy that daddy only gave me sixpence. He shakes his head.

"Tell your daddy he's a terrible man!"

"Well," daddy says. "How did you get on?"

"He says you're a terrible man."

"Good, he smiles. "Here's the thrupence you saved. That's the way you bargain!"

MAMMY'S NAME IS CATHERINE, but everybody calls her Ciss. She was born on a farm in Billeady, Co. Monaghan on the twenty-seventh of March 1904, the last of six girls, no boys. Her parents were that worried about her that she was baptised in Annyalla church the same day. And imagine – she used to walk six miles a day, barefoot except in winter, to her school in Lackagh. She wasn't like daddy: she loved school and her teacher, Miss Connolly. Her sister Margaret sent her money from America to go to Hughes' Academy in Belfast and learn about business. The Tower in Clones gave her her first job. Next she started her own small shop and eating-house in Meeting House Street in Keady. She would give dinners to people coming in to the Friday Fair for the pig market. That's where she met daddy. The first day she served him, she and her sister Margaret came out of the shop to look up the street after him because he said he was a tailor but was wearing green trousers and a jacket that didn't match!

When she was twenty-two she joined her sisters in Providence, Rhode Island, then on to New York to Maceys Department Store. From Maceys she remembers cheering a man called Lindberg after he had flown across the Atlantic and she remembers people ruined by a great 'depression' in 1929. At weekends she worked as a servant with her cousin in one of the big houses in Long Island.

One of my mother's guest teas: she is in the middle at the front.

I think she's famous all over Armagh for the things she learned in America, not just about running a business but especially for her gingerbread cake and her mock-lobster sandwiches. Every now and again she organises Ogle Street and Thomas Street guest teas and whist drives to raise money for the missions and she says people can't get over her food.

"Oh, they knew how to eat in the big houses in Long Island. You wouldn't find Heinz Salad Cream there. Always Hellman's Mayonnaise. And no mince-meat either, nor tinned stuff."

I know she's right, but I tasted tinned beans one day and I wish we bought them the odd time, even if they're bad for me.

Mammy came home after five years in America with five hundred pounds and she married daddy that year, in 1931. They had their wedding breakfast with a small number of family and friends at the White Horse Inn in Drogheda. They stayed there that night for their honeymoon.

They tell me daddy sold a cow and his motor-bike when he got married and they rented 13 Ogle Street. There mammy set up a sweet-shop and grocery. Under the front counter she later kept smuggled goods – butter and sugar and tea – for 'special' customers. Daddy did his tailoring up the back. Manys a time people who bought suits needed shirts and shoes, and mammy spotted her chance – she switched to drapery in 1933. Next, she rented number ten across the street and started another shop, just for babies and children. Daddy didn't agree, but auntie Margaret backed her and mammy moved across with the family to number ten. Daddy wouldn't move for a month, then gave in.

Sometimes mammy stops men bringing parcels from the back of the shop where daddy works. She asks for a receipt, for she knows daddy has a soft heart, that people spin sad stories to him and he says they can pay later. Still, mammy is generous when people are in real trouble.

"You can't run a business if you let people pull the wool over your eyes," she tells the staff. Helen Brennan works in the baby shop and she says the people of Armagh wouldn't have shirts on their backs only for the goodness of the Quinns.

Mammy says we're poor. "We're not rich," she says. "We can't afford a car. I don't know where we'd be only for Frank Toner's taxi to take us to visit my sisters of a Sunday."

I wonder why we're not rich – mammy has near three thousand club customers paying money every week to the club collectors, and we sell lots of clothes at Easter and Christmas and First Communion and the close of the Mission.

"But sure I have to give the club customers a shilling in the pound off everything they buy, and I have to pay the club collectors and all the staff – in the coats and dresses department, in the underwear and wool department, the shoe department, the boys departments, the baby shop..."

"You couldn't make money if you tried," daddy says, "with all the expenses facin' you."

I worry that there won't be enough to feed us some day. Though I still steal from the till.

One of our top collectors for the shop club is Mrs Pettigrew. She's a stout wee woman with a headscarf covering her permed blue hair. She is a Protestant but her face looks as worn-out as a Catholic's. Daddy warns me to be polite to her and not to say anything.

"You don't open your mouth to her except hello."

"But I wouldn't talk about Protestants to her, daddy."

"Whisht! You don't talk at all. Silence is a virtue!"

On Saturday evenings, Missus Pettigrew appears in our dining-room bearing money, notebook and stories. She pulls off the headscarf and seats herself sideways at the table. Mammy spreads out the ledger and writes as Missus Pettigrew talks. I listen in as she tells why one Missus is only paying a shilling this week but will be back to one and sixpence next week now that the coal bill is paid. Another Missus "got her leg broke stepping off a stool and won't be paying you nothin' more till she's better. You want to see her, Missus Quinn, she was the picktur' a' death."

Mammy notices me listening and sends me up the stairs to bed.

MAMMY SOMETIMES TAKES THE TRAIN up to Belfast on Wednesdays to buy stock for the shop. An odd time she takes me with her. The window of the train is a magnet for me with a million things charging past it. Sad back yards, stuffed bins, tidy clothes lines, the backs of poor little houses that I'd hate to live in, then a broad forest of trees chased by a sudden blur of up-close grassy banks. And all the time telegraph poles streaking after one another faster than my eyes can catch. I put my fingers out to feel the blast until mammy tells me to close the window and not let in the cold.

In Belfast I traipse around after mammy all day. The warehouses are dull: just doors off cobbled streets and up old stairs to huge rooms with a damp cloth smell and row after row of dresses, coats, blouses and skirts. Shelves piled with parcels clutter the walls. A jumble of bulky cartons fills open spaces on the floor. Bustling men stop to switch on smiles at mammy. Some are 'travellers' who visit our shop with cases of samples and are usually given tea and buns.

"Missus Quinn, a pleasure to see you! You're looking so well. How are you? And is this your little man? I'm sure he's a great help to you today."

They wink-wink to mammy at the idea of me helping, and they smile grins at me. I can't help being proud of how popular mammy is.

AT CHRISTMAS WE HAVE A PARTY in the dining-room with its cosy low ceiling. The gas heater gurgles softly and the flickering blue gas light makes the spread of sandwiches and lemonade sparkle on our folded-back table. We can stay up late tonight. Everybody sings or says a poem. I sing 'My Lagan Love' and get claps. You have to coax Mrs Starrs because she says she can't sing, then she plays the piano and sings 'The Boul' Fenian Men.' Everybody says what a nice voice she has. It is mammy, though, who makes my head and my heart swell with her Italian and Jewish accents in the poem 'Kelly's Dream.' I swim in her conquering glory.

SHADOWS AND SUNLIGHT

Some of the maids who look after us have been kind,
Sara Cashin, Nellie Doran, Rose McHugh. Not Ivy.
She wears black clothes, sort of like a witch. She
darkens a room when she walks in. She darkens my
life.

I'm late, and I pull Victor and Eugene home,
bossy the way I'm bossed. Ivy pounces at the door.

"What kept yiz? Dawdlin' home from school! I'll
teach yiz to dawdle! Up the stairs! All up the stairs
an' take your pants down!"

"Aw, please, Ivy! We won't be late any more.
Please..."

Begging never changes her mind, makes her
more cruel.

"Did you hear me?" Her voice muffles me. We
kneel together in a row, bare-bottomed, stifling sobs,
whimpering, our bodies bent over the bed as she
commands.

She takes a wooden coat-hanger from the
wardrobe.

Four-year-old Eugene first. He screeches and
jumps up at the first shock of pain. Turning his
bottom away makes her angrier and she hits him
anywhere on his thighs and legs, even his penis. He
jumps around with the agony and the effort to avoid
her until she orders him into the other bed and he
dances on his bottom, all dignity robbed, in under the
bedclothes.

Any pity I feel for him is choked by fear for myself. Waiting increases the torture. I think she knows that.

Now Victor. From yowling to yells and bawls. He turns, arms stretched down over his knees like a monkey, but she pushes him off balance back on the bed and lashes wildly with the hanger at his thighs and bum. "I'll teach you to stay where I told you," she snarls, her teeth bared.

Now my turn. She holds me down to stop me jumping away and my trapped legs quiver up and down in kicks of agony as she welts my bum. I have no more dignity than a dog. I howl and screech my begging. I am not even trying to be brave, but I hate her with my worst hate. I imagine her big ugly bum going to the toilet. It is a sin to think like this, but I don't care, it is my only way to hate her back from beneath my squeals.

THE CHOIRBOYS HAVE A PARTY at Christmas and a trip to Butlin's in the summer, so I join. I walk to the practice on Thursday evenings and dilly-dally home. "They kept us late," I say. I like being out in the streets as late as eight o'clock.

Dickie Doh Holden runs the choir. They say he's ninety years old, but he can make the organ bellow into the roof of the cathedral and send thunder crashing round the pillars. Sometimes the thunder reaches inside me and lifts my spirit, but mostly I'm bored with the long Mass on Sundays. At least it's better up in the choir gallery. I can whisper to the boy beside me. We tell each other who our daddies and big brothers can beat up. I read the writing on women's headscarves and look down at the oddness of bald heads, one of them with a dent in it. I wonder was the man born like that or did he fall? I day-dream.

The altar boys also have a party once a year, so I join. Mammy says it's a privilege to be on the altar so close to the priest. It's scary for a dreamy person like me – sometimes I forget to ring the bell or fetch up the wine and water. Priests are very serious and have special smells and sounds and they mutter at the altar – it's part of being holy.

One day I serve a private Mass for Father Starrs. There is no one in the church except mammy and Mrs Starrs, just the two for communion. I put out the communion cloth on all the altar railings, maybe fifty yards of it. I see a corner I missed, rush back and fix it. I don't know why Mrs Starrs and mammy are giggling. I'm supposed to cover all the railings: that's the rule.

I AM EIGHT years old. A magnet draws me. Leo Cowan's bright red magnet is horse-shoe shaped and can latch on to the iron legs of a desk. Strange, it won't lift brass thrupenny-bits, but it grabs up nibs and thumb tacks, even a pen-knife. I must have it.

Stealing is easy. I'm used to taking what I want. I wait till the end of the school day, move in, and it's mine. No remorse. As I walk home with Victor and Eugene, I delight in the thrill and the newness of the magnet in my right-hand pocket. Just one dark thought: what if Ivy – invading, suspicious, pocket-pouncing Ivy – finds my new toy? The lies that fool others don't fool her. Excitement shrinks to fear. I must hide the magnet. Hiding it happens like stealing it. I look for my brother Eugene's open jacket pocket and drop the magnet in out of sight.

When we arrive home, Ivy is busy. She ignores us until Eugene finds a magnet in his pocket and is fool enough to take it out in amazement, wondering where it came from. I disappear up the stairs. Ivy is a cat with a trapped mouse. She knows about things, she says, especially lies. She knows his pretend surprise for the lie it is. He better stop telling lies or she'll make it worse for him. She knows what a dirty little liar and thief he is at five years old and she doesn't want to think what he'll be like when he's older. Where did he steal it? Own up now. Now, or he'll get the worst beating of his life. A stick comes out because a stick is what's needed to deal with lies and stealing. Now will he tell? I hear cries, more threats, now animal screaming. Eugene is being walloped with the savage strength of God-backed right confronted by evil. My youngest brother, innocent, five years old, getting my beating.

I stand stuck to the top step of the stairs listening to the screams. Poor Eugene. His bellows and yells of pain echo into my chest and quiver through my belly. I can't own up. I won't.

CHRISTMAS IS THE MOST MAGIC time of the year. For weeks the ceiling of our shop is dressed in twirled, whispery, coloured paper that flutters and dances when the door opens. Curls of berried holly smile into the street from our shop window. Dots of cotton-wool drizzle snow down the edges. All through our house the holy pictures and framed photos have a scarf of holly. When the Christmas tree goes up my heart surges.

Christmas Eve is filled with longing. I am warm inside with love for Santa Claus and we get nuts going to bed. I hang my stocking at the bottom of the bed for Santa to stuff presents into it. I must be asleep when he comes. I lie awake for hours, my eyes shut tight. My older sisters know bold children who woke up Christmas morning to coal in their stockings. Imagine. Dirty coal. I'm bad on the inside, mostly good on the outside. I'm hoping Santa doesn't know about the bad.

I wake up early Christmas morning and creep across the bed to explore Santa's presents. Good, there is an orange, a pencil, a rubber and a bar of Cadbury's Fruit and Nut in the stocking. Now the big present. My heart chills. First at Santa's writing on the brown paper parcel, 'To Michael and Victor, love Santa.' I want something that's mine, not shared with somebody who's stuck on to me. The second chill is the present – a thing for tracing animals and birds. Eugene gets the soldiers and red Indians and green cardboard fort that I want. With my new pencil and rubber I change the names around. Eugene and Victor get the tracing toy and I get the fort. No one will know. I'm wrong – mammy and my sisters know my writing and see the smudges where I rubbed out names. Everybody scolds me and is cross. At least that's better than a beating. I'm sorry. Sorry I left smudges, and that they knew my writing.

THEY TAKE MY TONSILS OUT when I'm eight. Proudly I wear a scarf that tells the street, "This is the boy that had an operation in the hospital." When the scarf comes off, I have a more important thing wrong with me: pleurisy. At Lurgan hospital Nurse Wiley loves me, and I get Beanos, Dandys, Lucozade and grapes from home. I have come out of the side-wings onto a bright stage. I don't want the lights to fade.

They don't fade. Mammy says I need country air to recover and they deliver me in a taxi to her sister in Derrynoose. I am in an open farmhouse filled with the presence of calm, stout Auntie Margaret. Chatty girl-cousins, years older than me, are welcoming and kind to me. Grown-up men gather in to the big kitchen in the evening for 'talk.' When they hear of something good, bad or wonderful, they shake their heads and agree, "Well, tha's a terra! Man dear, a holy terra!" I am talked to like a grown-up and trusted with a candle going up to bed. There is a dog here to race through a field with, and wary hens at squawky peace, and a donkey and cart to ride with Gerry to the bog in. There are cats daring you to chase them. There is hay in the barn to bounce and float on, and a special smell of rot in the flaxholes. I have tea and soda bread with the men by the ditch of a hayfield. All by myself I watch clouds shaping and reshaping and see misty drizzle in the evening that drips through the hedges with a soft silence.

Auntie Margaret has a small country shop that she set up with her money from working in America. Three afternoons a week, Harry Corr the breadman delivers fresh brown-roofed batch loaves to us. I wait for him. You're supposed to call grown-up people 'mister,' but Harry is just 'Harry.'

"Hello, Harry. Did you think I'd maybe be gone back home to Armagh?"

"No, sir-ee, son. No, sir-ee! A wee birdie tol' me you were still here up to yer mischief, an' I was to have a bun kep' for ye!"

I don't believe a bird really told him, but how could I not love Harry when he rolls out an extra shelf in his van and hands me a sugar-topped, penny 'Paris Bun.' I sit on the stone steps of the barn and nibble all around the edges to make the bun last.

One day my tongue is caught in a kitchen fork.

"Pull it! Pull it! Pull it off quick," uncle Johnny splutters

My cousin Betty holds him back, works at the fork and frees my tongue. Uncle Johnny can't stop muttering, grumbling at the threat to a child in his house. He wants to put all the kitchen forks into a potato bag and bury the bag in a field. They talk sense to him. I'm shocked: somebody sees me more important than all the forks in the kitchen.

Another day they don't see me in the yard and a big cart of hay tilts on top of me. The dead load of two haystacks crushes my chest and mouth into the stone street of the farmyard. Men and women fork the weight off me in a panic and I rise up out of the hay a celebrity, the centre of conversation and concern for a few days. I remember the fuss and the attention better than the gasping for breath.

The Clarkes think I'm funny, that I say cute, towny things. From the bedroom upstairs I hear them repeat my deeds of the day, laughing. Tomorrow I will say more funny things.

Birds used to perch on Saint Francis' shoulders and wild animals felt safe beside him. I envy him. I imagine birds on my shoulders: boys are amazed to see a wren eating out of my hands. They recognise my holiness in the miracle of a fearless wren.

My cousin Eileen says it's easy to catch a bird: you sprinkle salt on its tail. Getting close is the hard bit. One day I'm collecting eggs and see a wagtail fluttering, trapped in Auntie Margaret's henhouse. I rush to the house for salt, almost speechless. Eileen is not there. The others don't know about birds and salt. They laugh at me. It takes urgent, scarce minutes to convince them. I return to the henhouse with my salt, but the wagtail has gone. I was so close to catching a wild bird.

Chickens are different. The Clarkes have chicks and pullets and hens. You call "Chuckie-chuckie-chuckie" and they come crowding, stupid, greedy for scattered corn. I feed the young pullets in the wire cage. They are easier to catch than hens, trapped already. I have power over them. I can be kind or cruel. I lift the cage at one side. A curious pullet pokes its head out under the cage wall wondering about the grass outside. Mistake. I let the wall down on its neck, pleased with my trap. I meant to frighten it, but it's dead. Auntie Margaret mustn't find out that I'm a bad boy on the inside, so I rush in to tell about an accident to the pullet when I was giving it 'fresh air.'

I am not a Francis with animals. I torture a cat in a barrel of water, and I beat a whimpering dog in the barn, irked that it tries to escape.

AFTER SIX WEEKS I am back home with keen memories of being noticed and cared about. I am a character now, whose wise country sayings win me laughs.

Fourth class at school is a prison after Derrynoose. I test Brother McQuillan, tearful, fretting that my 'pleurisy pains' have come back. He stands on my wings.

"Quinn, what you have is an acute attack of Imaginitis!"

ONE SUMMER we take a train to Letterkenny. We shift cases and bicycles onto a bus and travel to Eddie Gillespie's guest house and forge in Derrybeg.

"You'll see the real Donegal soon," Gabe says, "all heather and rocks and mountain and no trees and the smell of turf."

I am in love with it. I leap across boggy heather and bare rocks and think I am the first person to tramp here since the very start of the world. I stand in sunshine listening to quaint insects chattering their delight to me. I love the feeling of aloneness in the silent, still long-ness of a valley under Muckish. I sing, and listen to the distant echo. I cackle into the echo, happy as a hen gloating over a new egg.

In Donegal I have adventures. Two days I spend with Victor fighting the charging brown current of a bog-water stream. We part-block it with sods from its bank packed into water-beaten stones. The stream bends sideways, cursing for six yards. I am as fulfilled as daddy knocking down the wall to extend the shop.

Near Magheragallon beach I ask mammy, "Are we allowed to go wild yet?" I race across short, tough grass onto a half mile of beach. I examine bits of worn-out, washed up wood. I wonder about the people long ago on a far-away island who maybe touched this wood. With my heels I ruffle the wavy ripple shapes in the sand. We pick stranded cockles and gather ragged lumps of turf to light a fire and boil a tin bucket of cockles in sea-water. As the water heats, the cockles rouse and stir and gape open.

Mammy spills them across the grass and we feast, gorging on them. Afterwards I sit still to watch the gulls. Inside I soar and dip and sail and skim with them.

When it rains, I spend a day in Gillespie's forge, allowed to blow the bellows that turn iron horse shoes white in the flames. In the dim forge I am enchanted and soothed by the clink-clank of the anvil and the murmuring of men speaking Gaelic. I breathe in the turf smoke and the smell of burning hoof and the pleasure of being accepted into the company of grown-up people, no longer a child to be 'seen but not heard.'

THE MISSION IS COMING. For weeks the priests remind us:

"There'll be a week for the men and a week for the women. I want you all out for Mass and a short sermon in the mornings and Benediction with a longer sermon in the evenings. No excuses now! If you can only come on a stretcher, come anyway!"

Everyone laughs. I look around me, shocked. You're not allowed to laugh in the church. It must be okay when the priest makes a joke.

Every morning and evening daddy and me and my brothers go early to get a seat in a crowded Saint Malachy's. One missioner is dull and serious. Two tell stories, and the stories hold me.

"My good men, there was a certain man who abandoned his holy Catholic faith. For forty years he mixed in bad, lewd company and lived an evil life. Never did he darken the door of a church on Sunday mornings: instead he lay in the sleep of sloth. Imagine the state of soul of that unfortunate wretch, my dear brethren, doomed to the eternal fires of hell where there is not even a drop of water to relieve the unending pain. The moment of his death drew near. His good wife stormed heaven with her prayers, but he stubbornly refused to change. Prayers are very powerful, however. As this poor man sank towards death, his wife's earnest prayers were answered and the miracle occurred. He turned in the bed and asked for a priest. I am happy to tell you, my dear men, that this man made a good and sincere confession, his soul was wiped clean of all those foul sins and he was anointed with the Last Sacraments. That man died in the deep peace of God twenty minutes later and was received into the loving arms of Jesus. I have no doubt he is in heaven now, enjoying the everlasting bliss of God and His holy angels."

Gosh! He was lucky. How could he have been so blind for so long! I like hearing true stories like this. I hope everyone else in this church is listening and will change their minds if they're tempted to give up their faith. I absolutely wouldn't. One of the missioners spent a whole frightening sermon on hell and it would put you off mortal sins. I don't commit mortal sins myself, and I definitely won't start now.

The women's mission is next. One of the busiest times of the year in our shop. There is the same excitement about the Sunday afternoon 'close of the mission' as there was about Easter bonnets. Even poor customers are borrowing from the shop club to buy new coats and frilly hats with more feathers and flowers than hat. Mammy has her hair permed and is wearing a hat decorated with pretend fruit in red and green and yellow.

"Well, of course I have to be properly dressed up or what will people think about the clothes in my shop?"

I DON'T LIKE IT when the boys call me 'Quinn the Bin.' If you don't work at school, you could end up as a bin-man. I don't know what I'll be. Not a bin-man. There aren't that many jobs I know about. A girl can be a teacher or a nun or a nurse. A boy can be a teacher or a priest, not much else, especially not a doctor – that's for upper-class people. Being a priest is the best thing to be. I'd like that: everybody would love me being kind to them, especially mammy. It's out for me, though – you have to learn Latin. Maybe I'll be a Christian Brother. They take you early. Something in me would love to get away from home, away from the smallness and dullness of this Armagh hill.

An odd Sunday night there's a film at the Cosey Cinema, usually the life of a saint, to make money for the missions. The throat-stopping generosity and devoutness of Saint Bernadette and Saint John Bosco stirs a part of me and lifts me. They make up my mind: I want to be a saint. I tell nobody: you're not supposed to want that – it's a sin of pride. I still steal, a lot more money now, and I cover it up with lies. Saints don't steal or lie, they're perfect, but that's the path I'll take: I'm just postponing it, not ready yet.

BROTHERS AND MASTERS teach me for seven years at Greenpark. Some are kind, especially Brother Sullivan and Mr Toman. Most are cross. Everyone gets slapped, even if it's not fair. I don't tell the grown-ups at home: they'll say I must have deserved it.

A new Brother from Cork takes fifth class, 'Big Sully,' short for O'Sullivan. He is tall and handsome and terrifying. When Sully punishes you, he reaches for a cane or strap or stick and his face darkens. I cringe, shrinking into my desk watching. He swings all of his six foot height and weight into a monster lunge that lifts his feet off the floor as he stabs the tips of your fingers. If you pull the fingers back, his anger swells and he doubles the slaps. He forgets he's hitting a boy. Quigley in my class runs away from the beating, hitching lifts with his wee brother piggyback. The police catch him in Omagh. Now he is walloped in front of the class, six of Sully's plunges onto each hand every half hour for half a day. I cower, numb with fear and with pity for him.

I don't hate Big Sully as the other boys do. I am scared of his temper and I also love him. I'm his pet. He gives me jobs to do like posting his letters. I glow when he takes me on his knee in front of the class. He doesn't see through me, doesn't know about me being bad inside.

Grown-up men also love Sully for bringing hurling to the town. He tells us Christy Ring is the best hurler Ireland ever had. He must be.

The Beano comic gives me an idea. Dennis the Menace celebrates April Fool's Day by pinning 'Kick me hard' to the back of his teacher's gown. I'll do that on Sully!

There is a titter when Sully writes on the blackboard. He turns and glares, the face dark, then gropes to find the card pinned to his soutane. His eyes blaze. He blares:

"Stand up the boy who did this!"

I rise up flustered, quailing, stuttering, "Sir-sir... April Fool!"

"Not funny, Michael Quinn!" he sputters. "Not funny at all! I am surprised at you!"

I suffer no other punishment, but I will leave it to Dennis the Menace to play his own tricks in future.

AT AGE NINE I sit the eleven plus exam to transfer into secondary school. I fail. I don't mind, I'm young enough to do it again. It'll be another year with my hero, Sully. I am shocked when a boy in Dobbin Street who failed is given a flailing by his daddy.

The second time I pass, sit an exam for Saint Patrick's College and win a scholarship to go there.

I am looking forward to the change, to going off boarding to the College. I wonder who will be my friend?

IMPRISONED IN SAINT PAT'S

ARMAGH HAS TWO HILLS, each crowned with a cathedral. In 1952, eleven years old, I move to the other hill as a boarder. Three buildings are stamped on the hilltop: the stone residence of Cardinal McRory, Primate of all Ireland; the Catholic cathedral that frowns across at the Protestant one; and the grey spread of St Patrick's College. For six years the cathedral clock next the college hammers out triumphant church gongs every quarter hour, and on Sundays Dickie Doh Holden belts cheerful mediaeval chimes across the Armagh countryside.

I am uniformed in grey trousers and a black blazer bearing a red cardinal's hat on the pocket. I wish it was new, not Pat's old one. Mum says I'll grow into it.

"You'll be off the streets, protected from bad influences," she says. "You'll have morning prayers and morning Mass and evening prayer and study time. It's a great chance for you."

I discover that the College is a 'minor seminary,' ambitious to turn out clerical students for the priesthood.

I stock up for my new life by stealing two pounds from the shop till. Mum and dad deliver me up to the Dean, Father Devine. A prefect takes over, Liam Wilson, respectful and quiet. We are given beds in the first-year dormitory on the top floor. God, I'm going to have to take off my clothes tonight in front of all these boys. I unpack into my locker and shelf and chat to the boy next to me, Peter Gilmore from Magherafelt.

"Do you know where Magherafelt is?"

"Aw yeah," I lie.

"What soccer team do you support?" he asks.

"Ahhh... No team in particular," I mumble.

A SHRILL ELECTRIC BELL summons us to the refectory. Down four flights of stairs we trundle past high windows filled with cathedral. Over a hundred shoes make a new sound, clattering on the steps and rumbling through a long, hollow corridor decorated with decades of Gaelic Football teams. Through the swinging doors of the ref we stream into a hall full of green formica tables. We wait, standing. Quiet spreads. Only the cawing and bickering of crows outside. The Dean begins.

"Bless us, O Lord, and these Thy gifts which of Thy bounty we are about to receive through Christ Our Lord, Amen."

Another new sound: the sudden gabble of a hundred boys chattering and of metal chair legs raking the hard floor. There is a plate of bread on the table, two slices each, a metal jug of milk, one round pat of margarine per boy and a large dented metal teapot. We're on rations after the war. Scarcity doubles my appetite.

After tea there's 'recreation' in the back field, a lone priest on guard. I stand at the path with new boys. Peter Gilmore says he has a brother, Gerry, also in first year. I announce that my two brothers have been here. Nobody heeds me.

I learn new words: sweets or food from your home is 'grub'; to ask for grub is to 'mooch'; first years are 'preps'; to 'scoot' a prep is to exercise seniority by clearing him off the handball alley or off a bench where he is playing push-penny with a comb and coins along the wooden seat. To tell tales on someone is to be a lousy 'rubberneck.' The toilet is the 'jacks,' its cubicles are 'horse-boxes' and toilet-paper is 'bumph.' One poor lad is nicknamed 'Bumph.' Some of us preps have already been given nicknames. Peter Gilmore's is okay – 'Pipsqeak.' I'm scared of a nasty one. My brother Gerard had limped with a broken leg in first year and became 'Silver' after one-legged Long John Silver. A few seniors remember him and call me 'Silver.'

Some second years hover around a long-handled iron pump that squeaks and groans when it doles out drinking water.

"Watch out," I'm warned, "They're on'y waitin' 'till the Dean is off his guard. They want to 'duck' us preps, baptisin' us into this place."

I avoid the ducking – just luck. I do not avoid a 'stroke on the stern' (a full strength whack from behind on an unsuspecting bum, which amuses everyone but the victim).

Before bed we congregate for night prayer in the chapel, preps at the front. Silence after that. The prefect puts out the lights. I whisper a while to Peter Gilmore. He's friendly. I might be pals with him. But I know nothing about soccer: I'm boring.

AT HALF SIX the bell blares to get up. We tumble out to cold-water washbasins and into uniforms. Vincentian priests run the school and one says Mass. We mumble responses in Latin.

Bread and marge for breakfast, but every second morning there's a short sausage, a 'pop,' or a slice of fried bread, 'dip.' They become a form of currency: "I'll give you half a pop for that."

The electric bell shrieks through the day. Into classrooms now to strange books being distributed. Father Kenny takes us for Latin. Amo, amas, amat… How did the Romans grapple with this weird grammar? How could they follow such a complicated language? I can't grasp this talk of 'temporal clauses' and 'adjectival clauses'? How is it the other boys are catching on? I am drowning, sinking to the bottom of the class. I look at the clock. I dream about a Cadbury's fruit and nut bar. I study the back of one boy's head, the hair bush-like, a cow's tail standing up at the crown. Has he forgotten to comb it or does he just not care? Another fella's hair is glossed with Brylcreem. I must ask my mum to bring me up some. Amamus, amatis, amant…

The Dean, Father Devine, teaches history. No history this first day, just shepherding us through the book of College Rules. We will be expelled for going down town without permission, for stealing, for impure actions. There is a Latin prayer to Our Lady to keep us pure, 'Maria, mater gratiae.'

After classes, there is meat, turnip and soggy potato followed by a lump of rice pudding. The boy beside me can't eat the rice and gives me half a bowl of it. I gobble it, eager as a dog.

We tog out for Gaelic football. Wet, cold football. Worse than Latin. I run wherever the ball runs and stumble around it, confounded, when it strays near my two left feet.

"Quinn! Quick! Here!"

I kick it forward to Tommy Savage.

"What the hell are you doin'? He's on the other team, you fool!"

A fool! They don't pass the ball to me anymore. I'm cold. And useless...

After a shower, we tramp up to the study-hall, a great rectangular room crammed with a hundred and forty desks in seven rows. Seniors at the back, preps at the front. I tidy my new books and close the lid. A dead hour and a half here. I grapple with Latin homework, geography, Irish, religion... I wish my handwriting wasn't squiggly. I dream of roughing my way past puzzled players to an astonishing goal. Crowds cheer me.

From time to time, the teacher on duty at the back prowls down an aisle. He swoops on a senior reading a comic and mutters at him as he confiscates it. We look around from the front.

"Get on with your study!" he glowers at us.

Bread and marge again for tea-time, followed by half an hour in the back field, a long hour in the study-hall, night prayers and bed.

THERE ARE FOUR LAY TEACHERS, all of them draped in gowns that billow through the corridors. Master O'Boyle ('oul' Sean') takes us for Irish and Geography. Cords of frumpy hair peep like sheeps' eyebrows over a high shining forehead. His trousers sag into his laces and his tie floats out over a bulge at his belly. His eyes look flat and weary, yet he is jovial and earthy in the classroom.

"Open Rasper at page twelve!"

The author of our geography book is Jasper with a J, but Sean is aware of the college slang, where a 'rasper' is a frequent farter.

"Chancellor, can you not find page twelve yet? Maybe, son, you might consider takin' up plumbin'!"

Sean spends holidays and weekends collecting Ulster folk-songs for a weekly BBC radio programme. I suspect he'd prefer that to being stuck here. Even in class he sometimes bursts into song. He tells us what's good folk music and what's awful. I'm proud to have somebody important teaching us, but I don't understand when he explains longitude and latitude, and I find Irish almost as knotty and taxing as Latin. I sense that I'm going to fail both Geography and Irish.

Master Forde ('Bucky') has us for French. Another impossible, thorny language! We still have a choice of French or Science. I ask if I can switch. Yes, there's room in the new science lab.

Johnny Doherty ('Johnny Nyark') teaches science. A nyark is a nagger. Sometimes the boys sing, "Johnny Nyark goes nyark, nyark, nyark-alum, all day long" to the tune of 'The Wipers on the Bus.' Actually, he doesn't nyark that much and I enjoy doing experiments alongside brainy Harry the Horse

Toner. Nobody realises until the Christmas exams that Harry has been doing all the calculations for me. By then I have missed too much and hit the bottom of the class in yet another subject.

No teacher uses a strap or cane. If we break a rule or fail to do a homework, they send us to the Prefect of Studies, Father Kenny. We meet him before lunch.

"What did you do wrong?"

I tell, and get two slaps with the strap. Sore, but not heavy. His eyes are kind and fair.

I'LL FIND A FRIEND. Someone who's about perfect. Maybe Peter Gilmore. He and his brother Gerry are popular. He's small, yet great at football, and he has a kind face. It's just... I'm not popular. I'm not sure anyone would like me if they knew me. There's nothing to me.

For a few days I rehearse my courage.

"Can I be your friend and walk round with you?"

"Yeah, sure."

I'm happy as a puppy. Playful. Delighted. After a week I can't keep it up. I don't know how to keep a friend. Anyway, Peter has flaws: his voice is squeaky. I'd rather be friends with his brother Gerry, tall, handsome, more serious.

I move to Gerry. Peter waits around, then strays to new friends.

I tire of Gerry. He's very serious, coughs in a funny way. He is flawed too. Will I ever find a perfect friend? I drift from Gerry.

I am alone. What was I thinking? I like Peter. Gerry too –such friendly lads. I don't know where to go, who to talk to. I act the clown , and the boys call me 'stunt.' Ugh! The thick sound of this new nickname. I escape to the chapel. God loves everyone. I don't have to make an effort here. I have a perfect friend. No flaws. Never trivial or squeaky. No annoying habits. Hours I spend looking at the gold door of God's little house behind the altar, watching the flickering flame of the oil lamp. I shelter before the plaster statues of Jesus and his mother, numbed to the misery outside. Paddy McIvor is eight benches in front of me, in silence, up closer to Jesus. They say Paddy saw Our Lady when she appeared in Ardboe. I wish I had seen her. I wonder if my presence in this holy place is making me a saint? If only I could work miracles and cures I would show them...

FATHER DEVINE is Dean of Discipline. A bit sarcastic, but generally fair. He uses the history class to nose us out.

"I want you each to write down what you think – who's the best sport in the class, able to take his beating..? Who's the worst sport..? Who's the most generous boy..? Who's the meanest..? Now pass the page to the boy beside you... We'll start with Desy Austin. Hands up, how many votes has Desy Austin got for best sport..? Worst sport..? Most generous..? Meanest..?"

Most boys pick up a ration of votes, except for generosity. I get twenty-two votes out of thirty-one. Father Devine notices me now. Generous. I am generous. Thankfully, nobody knows how I fund my generosity.

AFTER CHRISTMAS the exam results. I graze the bottom in most subjects. Thirteen out of a hundred in Geography. Father Duggan gives us the results in Geometry.

"In first place," (pause) "there's a fella called Jim Slevin. And a fella called Michael Quinn."

"Quinn is stupid. How did he get first?"

Solving maths puzzles is different: it stirs and energises me. Maths and English are oases, not new subjects. When I awaken, mornings, the other subjects loom to stir the dread in my stomach. In this Gaelic Football college, where the captains leave me standing, last picked, I am neither sporty nor brainy. And I am friendless. Trapped in a young boy's prison.

SPORTS DAY is in June. I'd love a medal, even third place. With stolen money I join every event, run all the races and jump high and long. I win nothing. That evening in the study hall Father Devine doles out the medals.

"And we have a special consolation prize tonight. It's for Michael Quinn who didn't win anything but who enrolled in every single event. It's people like Michael who make a sports-day successful."

I stumble up stunned to the front. He presents me with a brightly coloured tie. I'll keep this tie!

FATHER MURNAGHAN preaches a sermon:

"Stealing starts small. Little by little it grows bigger. It leads to lies as we try to cover it up. And more lies. And more stealing. Until we're caught in the grip of evil and it's harder and harder to escape..."

I sit alert, transfixed, as he talks. Yet, headlong as a train, I continue.

A boy in our dormitory has chocolate bars in his case. It's quiet when I enter the dorm at break-time. I open the locker. Damn, his case is locked! Will it break open? Close to the lock, I force the cardboard and tear a way in. I gather my plunder and hide it in my pillow.

"I will find the thief," Fr Devine says. "I'm going to ask each boy in this dorm if he stole the sweets. I'll know from your face who did it!"

"Was it you?" he repeats when he comes to me.

"No, father."

I sense my cheeks crimson hot. He passes. My brother Gerard is studying to be a Vincentian priest, so the Dean does not suspect me.

It is the end of term before I steal again. I wrap Peter Gilmore's stamp album into my towel. At home, I add his best stamps to my collection and burn his album.

IT'S THE SUMMER HOLIDAYS. I scent a bargain. If I sell a hundred and forty books of raffle tickets at half a crown a book, the organisers will give me a free Raleigh bicycle. Dad will buy twenty books if I sell the rest and choose a ladies' bicycle that my sisters can ride.

I hawk tickets to all the easy neighbours, local shopkeepers and relatives. Into the streets of Armagh I go then evening after evening through drizzle and downpour. I return late, clutching money and ticket stubs.

"You're frozen... How much money did you get..?"

"Over a pound."

"How did you sell that many..?"

"I got people comin' off the buses. That was the best place. An' comin' out of the pictures at the Ritz an' the Cosey."

"You're an amazin' man! Do you see this? Hasn't Michael some go in him. Look at all the tickets he sold! He'll get that Raleigh bike yet."

No one suspects my secret – my daily trips to the till in the shop where I steal the money for the tickets. I have not been braving the weather. I have spent my evenings in one of the three Armagh picture-houses to see the latest Holywood films. After a film I visit a telephone kiosk to copy names from the 'phone directory onto the ticket stubs.

A month later, I own a new Raleigh ladies bicycle and gain a reputation for enterprise and determination that I deserve. But not the way anyone imagines.

SECOND YEAR at the College. I'm in Father Devine's history class.

"Fifty years ago, a glass of whiskey cost a penny. That was all."

He told us this last week, also a few weeks ago. He mustn't know he's repeating himself. I put up my hand.

"Please, Father, you told us that twice before."

Silence. He stares at me a long moment.

"Yes, Michael Quinn! And I'll tell it to you again! You cheeky pup! Get out of this class and don't come back until I tell you!"

I rise aghast. Me cheeky? He mustn't have wanted to be told.

I wait outside, bewildered, quailing.

Shortly after the bell he emerges.

"Father..."

"Yes. What is it!" He looks through me.

"Father, I'm sorry."

"Well you might me!"

He bustles off abruptly, soutane swishing.

Some boys are amused. "Quinn, what did you say that for? You're a brave man, but you're an eejit. Didn't you know he would do his nut?"

I didn't know. How is it I don't pick up on things that are obvious to others?

IT IS THE CHRISTMAS HOLIDAYS and Orla Lennon is my first-ever girlfriend. I am twelve and she is five. She is dancing in a concert that my sister Anne is organising. Every evening I have to walk her home to the Mall. She holds my hand, a walking, talking, sparkling doll. I ache to live with her forever. With stolen money I buy her a bar of Cadbury's milk chocolate.

When the concert finishes I sometimes walk past her house, hoping to see her. Not a glimpse. She will never know of my love.

At the College, my affection is for boys. In the study hall I put apples or chocolate bars into the desk of a first-year boy I admire. When he finds them he turns and smiles. I smile back.

D'ARCY, THE FOURTH YEAR BULLY, pushes past me. I push back.

"Quinn, you're asking for trouble. Do you want to get your face smashed?"

"I'd like to see you doin' it."

"Right! Behind the jacks!"

Boys crowd around, smelling a fight, a diversion.

D'Arcy slams a single thick punch between my eyes. There is a flash, then darkness. I cannot see through the pain. Blood seeps from my nose. The fight is over – one blow. They cheer D'Arcy.

I don't understand why people bully. I would never bully. Being mean is different. I can't help being mean to my brother Victor. I'm a big third-year; he's just a first-year.

"Stay away from me! I don't want you near me. Don't even talk to me! Understand?"

Father Devine is still gathering information from the first years. He discovers that I have told Victor never to speak to me at school.

He knows I'm generous. I wish he didn't know about me being mean.

WE'RE GOING HOME tomorrow for Easter.

"First thing I'm gonna do," Tony Bradley says, "is sit me down to a big fry. Bacon an' egg an' dip an' two sausages. Naw, four sausages and two eggs. An' then... Then I'm gonna eat a load a' biscuits. An' brown lemonade. I can't wait, boy."

I can't wait myself, can hardly believe it. Home!

Hugs and kisses, a feed, a Biggles book upstairs in my room. Chats with Pat and my sisters.

Pat has read an article in the Reader's digest.

"It says some people don't like themselves, that they have an inferiority complex."

I can't look Pat in the eye.

"Oh... What does the man say about it?"

"He says you should stand in front of the mirror every morning and say, 'I like myself. I like myself. I really like myself.' And you need to keep repeating that during the day."

"Sounds a bit stupid!"

I look in the bathroom mirror.

"I really like myself," I say. My eyes wince. I cringe before the glass. A cold, scared look stares back at me. God! Do my eyes always stare like that? I would hate anyone to look at me that way.

"I really like myself, I really like myself, I really like myself..."

Aw, my nose, my big, ugly nose. I hate it. No girl is ever going to like me. Depression looks out of the mirror at me. Inferiority haunts me. I hate myself. I stand there five minutes, staring, hating, wishing...

During the day I repeat, "I like myself," but the Reader's Digest doesn't work, only reminds me how wretched I am.

I return often to the mirror, staring, hating, wishing...

The college is not my only prison.

ON A VISIT TO GERARD in Glenart, Wicklow, he asks, "How's school?"

"I hate bein' a boarder, Gerard... But I suppose it's okay."

It's not okay. Why do I say that? I'm miserable. I hate being near the bottom for nearly every subject. If I could be sick, I wouldn't have to do the exams. If I could break my leg or my arm. If I could cut my right hand.

I press a nail into the middle of my palm until the jab bites. Now put the nail on the desk and all I have to do is press my weight on it... It hurts. I'm not brave. I think I'll try it on my foot instead. If I jump on it my weight will force the nail in.

I take off my sandal, push the nail up through the sole and fasten the sandal back. Just one jump from the fifth step of the stairs, one second and it'll be over...

A quarter hour I hesitate, hovering at the brink, mustering courage, letting it drain off. I am a coward.

I plod a pass in my Junior exam at the end of third year, but school is still jail. I must escape.

"Dad, I want to leave the College. I'm no use at it. Can I not leave?"

"No. Look at your brother Pat. Turned his back on 'egucation' after Junior! Earns one pound seven and sixpence a week. You'll not be leavin' school, boy!"

"Could I even be a day-boy instead of a boarder? "

"No! That's the end of it! There's no more talk! Later you'll be glad."

My tears don't touch him. I must go back to the drudgery of Latin and Science and chasing a grim, thick football.

BEFORE THAT, I am home for the summer holidays, I read the Beano and Dandy comics. I read Enid Blyton and the Hardy Boys and my sisters' Schoolgirl Library Series. Then I discover Charles Dickens.

When dad sees me reading he doesn't find me a job in his tailor's den. "Good boy, I'll give you tuppence for every book you read."

But there's a cloud. The mother who was my bright sun is a disappointment, not perfect, flawed. She exaggerates her stories. She talks a lot about her health. When she complains about not being well, I look beyond at the wall and my eyes glaze over. She doesn't know about Geometry and the French Revolution and Charles Dickens: we have nothing in common. Kissing her is a duty.

My mother embarrasses me.

AWAKENING

I spend a month of the summer at the Irish College in Rannafast in lovely, rugged Donegal. Ten of us sleep in double beds in one house. We lounge across a bed playing penny-poker. We dander back and forward to the school together, shoulder one another into puddles, skim stones on the river. Easy friendships.

There are girls here who make my heart skip, like sleek, dark Sheila Devlin from Cookstown. Oliver Fields hints to her that I fancy her. She tells him okay.

"What can I do now, Oliver?"

"Aw, just take her to the back of a haystack and kiss her."

I seize up: the priests in Armagh say French kissing is a mortal sin. Nothing happens.

I share the bedroom with confident, full-of-music Phil Coulter from Derry. We're bound to win first place in the final *Coirm Cheoil* (concert). He composes *Nuair a Tháinig Rock 'n Roll go Rannafast*. (When Rock and Roll came to Rannafast.). He bounces onto the stage and Rock 'n Roll erupts into Rannafast. The students cheer. Seán Bán Mac Grianna, one of our teachers and brother of the writers Seosamh and Máire Mac Grianna, rises:

"Stop! Stop it! Stop!" he barks at us in Irish. "This song is sacrilege! Tonight you are destroying two thousand years of Irish culture!"

115

Next morning our course ends. I have relaxed in this careless ease, and I speak Irish better. A third subject to do well in at school.

BACK AT SAINT PAT'S, I join the compulsory Sunday afternoon 'walk' for all the boarders. A column of uniformed boys eels its way around the narrow streets of Armagh, a priest at the back flanked by two prefects. The procession reaches Ogle Street. I disappear in home for an unofficial twenty-minute food-visit before re-joining the straggling march on its return.

I wolf some food and await the returning students behind the front door of the shop. It's dark and quiet, a chance to attack the till. I pocket a ten-shilling note and a sheet of twelve postage stamps.

There is movement. Dad rises from behind the shop counter, silent. He holds out a hand for what I've stolen. I surrender my plunder and wait for the angry tantrum. Silence.

"How long has this been going on?"

I am too befuddled and naked to lie.

"For years... For years really."

"I see. Well, good may come from this now that you're finally telling the truth. But it's serious. Go now, but this is not the end. There will be drastic steps. I'll be telling the College president, the police, the local priests, your brother Gerard."

Dismissed, stunned, I join the returning walk.

For the next few days, out of contact from family and unsheltered in the rawness of boarding school, a hurricane of shock and fear rages through me. I am found out. What will happen to me? Will they expel me from the college?

A week later, I am home for Halloween, nervous, sobered. Dad talks on the phone to the police about me – I don't know that his phone is not engaged. I am disgraced, havocked – but thoughtful. Something happens – a shocked awakening, a dawn. Taking what belongs to another is twisted and wrong. I will never again take what does not belong to me. Never again.

MY BROTHER PAT looks out for me. At the age of fourteen, he takes me aside.

"Do you know about babies, where they come from?"

"Not really, no."

"The man puts his penis inside the woman and the seed goes inside her. Humans do the same as rabbits to have babies. Do you see?"

"Mm. I see."

I don't know what rabbits do. I don't ask.

Later I learn that a buck rabbit takes a female from behind. My breath stops when I imagine it. Wildly exciting, sinful, a bad thought, dirty… I won't think about it. It attacks me and I linger over it, almost helpless.

The priests warn us against sexual thoughts and actions. French kissing is a mortal sin. So is masturbation. I am too afraid of hell to do either.

I sit at the back of Latin class beside Peter Thorne. Father Doherty ('Wee Doc') is sitting helping someone near the front. Peter whispers:

"Michael, do you know how babies come out of their mothers' tummies?"

I whisper (this is close to 'dirty talk'), "I dunno, Peter... I think it's something to do with the belly-button."

"They could never fit out through there..."

"Yeah, I know. It's funny... I just don't know how it works... Unless it's out through their bottom... Nah, it couldn't be that either."

I AM FIFTEEN. I find I'm okay at the high jump and come second on sports day. I practice for the

Intermediate (under 16) mile race. Boys who know my weakness at football laugh. I run the mile in just over five minutes, breaking the school record. My name goes up on the framed Mile Records beside the footballers in the big hall. The glory!

Father Sheridan, the President, produces a play once a year. I am an old bed-ridden man wearing long johns in a Lady Gregory play, revelling in the limelight and praised for my performance. I have the main part in his next play, 'The Ringer.'

MY ENGLISH TEACHER is 'Baldy Curtain.'

"Your essay for this week is *How to make a bed*."

Boring! I decide to be the bed and I write what happens to me when people turn my mattress, thump me, shake the sheets over me, smooth me down.

"Quinn, you write well, but this is too imaginative. The examiner is not looking for imagination. He wants a beginning and a middle and an end."

Occasionally, though, I write a piece that he reads out to the class:

"Our house is stuck in at the back of four short streets, tucked in by chimneys, walls and trees. A long, winding shop twists out to stop suddenly in a façade of little shops that seem to prop one another up like a house of playing cards. Few know the boundaries of our intricate maze of backyards or the divisions of our solitary clothes line, and here, irrespective of County Council orders, we rule our little domains and run our tap waters at will…"

"Well done!" he says and shows my essay to other teachers.

School is different. I still hate football but the hours in the study-hall are contentment, luxury.

THERE IS A TWO-DAY SILENT RETREAT.

"Lads, this is a time when you let God speak to you. You must remain silent all day – at mealtimes, inside, outside, everywhere. Do not be a cause of distraction to other boys. And you may not read anything except these Catholic Truth Society booklets about the lives of the saints…"

We pack the silence with creative sign-language, clowning and amusing each another with raised eyebrows, puckered lips, monkey faces. Fingers wag in mock-warning; they point, curl, tap – or swish across a neck to notify, "You're dead, mister!" In return, arms tremble in mock-terror. Or we refuse to break the silence by mouthing words and lip-reading.

Twice a day there are sermons in the chapel. Slowly, more of us enter into the retreat. The short lives of the saints touch me: these giants of the spirit intrigue and grip me, become my heroes, my role models. After the retreat I read *Story of a Soul* and am charmed by the simplicity of St Therese's 'Little Way.'

I read more spiritual books, including Thomas Merton's *Seven Storey Mountain* about contemplation and prayer in a monastery. A monastic life attracts me. To be holy you need to get away from the world. You nearly have to be a priest...

I visit the college chapel, no longer to escape loneliness: I listen to God, who tells me to give back what I stole. Dad and mum forgive my debt to themselves and help me give money to charities when I don't remember the people I stole from. I tell Peter Gilmore that it was I had stolen his stamp album. He is shocked but magnanimous.

God wants me to be humble, to accept humiliation. In the Ritz cinema I pay sixpence instead of ninepence and am ushered to the front where only children and poor people sit. The embarrassment! I keep my head down while the lighting is on. I am not humble like St Therese.

DURING THE HOLIDAYS I glimpse girls who are like the Virgin Mary in the College chapel. I revere them from a distance, their beauty, virtue, mystery. I cycle past, brisk and nimble on my racer, pretending not to notice them. The bike keeps me safe from embarrassing myself before these virgin princesses.

At sixteen, the end of my fifth year at the college, comes another immaculate fairy, beautiful

Claire with long black eyelashes and full lips that everyone must long to kiss. I meet her on a summer course in Rannafast, dance with her at the céilís and play with her fingers as I walk part of the road with her to her house. On the way home from Rannafast I buy her a gold cross and chain in Letterkenny. Just before we part in Portadown I take a deep, nervous in-breath and give her my first kiss. She is not a good kisser. Her kiss is wet, not like my sisters' kisses, not like the pure kisses in the Schoolgirls Library series. Only afterwards does it strike me why she didn't keep her mouth closed. Now I would love to have sex with her. I dream about it but it's not allowed. I wish I was a Protestant – they seem to be freer about sex.

I'M IN MY FINAL YEAR, A-level, no longer a boarder, studying only History, English and Irish. I dislike the history classes for I don't relate well to the teacher. I have Jerry Hicks for both English and Irish. Gael-linn has just produced an LP record of his superb singing and he teaches Irish poetry by occasionally powering into song:

"You miss much of the poetry, lads, without the music."

He stands in front of the English class, looking silently, dramatically, at us until there is hush. A compelling actor, he brings out the satire in T S Eliot's 'Murder in the Cathedral' with a marvellously exaggerated English accent. He reads Chaucer with an earthy, almost-Cornish accent that alerts us to the realism and beauty of the poetry:

"Upon the cop right of his nose he hade a werte and thereon stood a tuft of heres, rede as the bristles of a sowes eres."

"You are the best pupil I have ever had," he tells me. "Not the most intelligent, but the one who soaks up things."

I love this man. I wish he was my father. At Christmas I am first in English.

At home I buy a great, bulky *Oxford Companion to English Literature*, start at page one and banquet on it in bed every evening. Thackeray, Charles Dickens, D H Lawrence and Thomas Hardy open new spreads of life before me. I savour Shakespeare, Alexander Pope, I read and re-read Charles Lamb's 'Superannuated Man.' English literature is wonderful.

THE COLLEGE PRIESTS make religion attractive. Fr Hederman is kind, inspiring, cares about us. We also have two newly-ordained priests, Fr Maher and Fr John Cleary, who are more like friends to me.

I confide in John Cleary that I have decided to be a priest.

"Think about being a Vincentian priest, Michael. You'll have a university education and you'll be leaving yourself open to different fields – working in a parish, going to Africa as a missionary, being a teacher in a secondary school, lecturing in Strawberry Hill or Drumcondra..."

"Okay. I'll go for the Vins then."

My mother is pleased.

THREE TIMES I HAVE BEEN ENTHRALLED by the film, 'The Student Prince.' The university students are so happy drinking beer out-of-doors and singing 'Gaudeamus igitur.' I can't wait to go to University!

I leave St Patrick's College in 1958 with a passion for English literature and a love of the Irish language and its traditional song. I am confused about sin, though, and feel guilty about sexual thoughts. I also have a fear of men in authority.

St Patricks College, the minor seminary for the archdiocese, entrenched on the other Armagh hill, is duly proud of me. Especially proud of all sixteen students from my class of thirty-one who have decided to become priests.

POSTSCRIPT

To everyone's surprise, not least Michael's, our little warrior did not turn out too badly in spite of his early forays into stealing and untruths. The boy who 'hated languages' became a teacher of Irish, French and Spanish for eleven years. The unhappy young Michael became a great deal more contented in himself, more appreciative of those around him and with a good sense of fun. He is particularly appreciative now of his siblings and of the goodness and dedication of his parents. He has been married to Terri for forty-five years, enjoys a happy marriage, and together they have reared their family in Newry. Michael founded a charity for parent education ("not a bad way to learn to be a better parent!") and in his retirement took time out from attacking briars in his garden to write this book.

Of the sixteen lads who opted to be priests, most, including Michael, left the seminary while still clerical students. Three remain priests.

Notes…

Notes…

Notes...

Notes…

Notes...

Notes…

Notes…

Printed in Great Britain
by Amazon